BEAST OF MAIN STREET

AMERICA'S MAIN STREET SPEAKS OUT ON COVID

MICHAEL SEAN COMERFORD

Published in the United States by Comerford Publishing LLC. at www. MichaelSeanComerford.com

Library of Congress Cataloguing-in-publication data.

The University of Florida's SPOHP's full video archive is at "Route Sixty-six Covid Oral History Project"

Reader Reviews are good medicine for the success of *Beast of Main Street*. Help give voice to the ordinary people living in extraordinary times. Please review at Goodreads or your favorite book buying site.

This book is dedicated to my daughter, Grace Comerford; to my parents, Gordon and Alice (Flatley) Comerford; and to my sisters Colleen, Maureen and Katie. To the ordinary people I met on Route 66 living in extraordinary times. And to luck!

"To bear in mind constantly that all of this has happened before. And will happen again—the same plot from beginning to end, the identical staging ... Only the people different."
– Roman Emperor Marcus Aurelius, *Meditations*, died of plaque.

"Sometimes in this life, under the stress of an exceptional emotion, people do say what they really think."
— Marcel Proust, author, *In Memory of Time Lost.*

"Nobody who has been through COVID will ever forget it ... COVID has changed the way we see the world."
— Bill Gates, founder of Microsoft and the Bill and Melinda Gates Foundation,. He is also a COVID survivor.

CONTENTS

"For there is no folly of the beast of the earth which is not infinitely outdone by the madness of men."
— **Hermann Melville, Moby Dick.**

"But no matter, the road is life"
— **Jack Kerouac, author of On The Road, which travels parts of Route 66.**

INTRODUCTION

JOURNEY BEGINS IN A DREAM

People and pandemics love roads.

The idea came to me in a dream. I only later realized what it was calling me to do.

I can't do it, there's a polar vortex outside.

Go.

I don't have a bicycle, camera, not even a winter coat.

Go.

I don't want to catch it, spread it or die.

Go. Go. Go!

So I set out to ask everyday people about what it's like for them to live in pandemic times. To listen to what people are really saying. Reflect on all I hear and see. And to get it all down before it gets remixed by memories.

I was unsure of the route but decided to ride 2,500 miles along Route 66 from Chicago to Los Angeles. The plan called for videotaping more than 100 people and posting it to a YouTube channel called *The Story Cycle*. My goal was to make most interviews short, to match the attention span of most people in this Information Age.

The American mountains, deserts, farmlands and cattle country became the backdrop as I crossed Illinois, Missouri, Oklahoma, Kansas, Texas, New Mexico, Arizona, and California.

Route 66 was chosen because it's a myth-making machine. It continues to inspire songs, movies, TV shows, and even a great American novel, *The Grapes of Wrath*, by John Steinbeck. He called it "the Mother Road." Its original chamber of commerce motto in the 1920s was "Main Street of America."

It's a road of fictions and legends. There's a faux history mixed with fiberglass giants, roadside dinosaurs, teepee motels, 1950's diners, and Route 66 murals the size of drive-in theater screens.

Yet there were real-time physical obstacles. I was 61 years old and out of shape. A brutal polar vortex caused power outages from the Midwest down to Texas. I waited until it passed, but snow was piled higher than trucks near my home.

My 16-year-old daughter, colleagues and friends told me not to go.

Too cold, they said. Too far. You'll spread Covid without knowing it. You'll catch it and die. All fears I had myself, after all, life's a gamble and I don't want to bet against the house on this one.

Route 66 isn't the best highway for bicycling in wind, rain, and snow. It's not even an official road anymore. The establishment of the Interstate Highway System in 1956 spelled the beginning of the end for Route 66, which officially ceased being a road in 1985.

Route 66 is now more of "way," as in the Apian Way in ancient Rome. It's a mix of two-lane frontage roads, main streets, and the remnants of the Historic Route 66.

I followed the Adventure Bicycling Association's official Route 66 corridor maps that run from Lake Michigan across and through the prairies, farmlands, small towns, big cities, the Mississippi River, the Ozark Mountains, the Continental Divide, the Colorado Plateau, the Mojave Desert, and on to the Pacific Ocean.

There was a sense of urgency too. I wanted to interview people while the pandemic was raging. The clock was ticking, and I thought I had to move fast before vaccinations or a change of seasons turned the pandemic into a memory.

I left in late February 2021 amid the greatest vaccine rollout in human history. The country was about to surpass 500,000 Covid deaths. Deaths were peaking at more than a 9/11 terrorist attack per day.

The numbers blurred the sense of lost individual lives. I wanted to talk to real Americans, individualistic, optimistic, contrarian, and sometimes a bit crazy. Most people weren't dying of Covid, and most people didn't know anyone who died of it.

News outlets were rightly focused on the deaths, but I needed to capture the zeitgeist of living in a pandemic. To discover the telling light in the crowd.

The country was bitterly divided over how to respond to the pandemic. Former President Trump's leadership was unclear, and many people conflated partisan politics with medical science. The January 6th riot and breaching of the US Capitol took place a month earlier. Newly elected president Joe Biden made it his goal to end the pandemic. Politics and the first inklings of vaccine hesitancy were high on people's minds.

I decided never to mention my politics, religion, or Covid opinions to people along the way. I never corrected facts or advocated for vaccinates.

In the interest of full disclosure, I feel I must reveal my connection to Route 66 and my bicycle of choice, the Pequod.

Shortly after my parents married, they hopped into an old Ford to drive from Wisconsin to San Diego, California, where my newly commissioned father was stationed in the navy. They spent a key portion of their honeymoon along Route 66.

I may have been conceived at one of the Route 66 motels now considered "classic." Talk about the Mother Road.

My bicycle has its own origin story. I once rode my new Panasonic bicycle to a Cubs game and locked it up to a "No Parking" sign in Wrigleyville. After the game, I returned to find the bike was stolen. That was 40 years ago.

I didn't have a bicycle when I decided to ride to California. I was forced to go pandemic shopping for a bike. Some bicycle shops had a year-long waiting list. I resorted to using the internet to search for a used bicycle.

A Polish immigrant on Chicago's North Side emailed me to meet him in a parking lot by a tire repair store. I'm sure it was all innocent, but the meeting felt clandestine.

I was waiting with my hands dug into my pockets when he rolled the bicycle around the corner. He was about my age and grew up under communism in Poland. His breath froze in mid-air.

"Two hundred bucks," he said in a thick accent. "Look. Original equipment. Is practically new."

The bicycle was the exact make and model of my stolen bike, along with the same black, padded handlebars. We were in Wrigleyville, within a short distance of the place my long-lost bike was last seen.

I'm not saying I bought my hot 40-year-old bicycle back from a North Side Chicago Polish immigrant. Neither am I saying that I was conceived in a cheap Route 66 motel. I am saying this life has a way of coming around full circle.

I named the bicycle Pequod after the ship in Herman Melville's *Moby Dick*.

The project's YouTube channel was *The Story Cycle*, so I laminated a three-by-two-foot sign for the back of my bicycle saying, "The Story Cycle: Tell Me A Story." I paid for business cards to hand out to skeptical interviewees.

A sign on the back of the bicycle and business cards were still not enough. I needed some gravitas. For that, I gained the support of the University of Florida's Samuel Proctor Oral History Program.

I filmed a personal commentary about the bicycle riding and local color in several states. I turned those "on the road" updates into short essays at the beginning of each chapter.

The essays tell stories about each state. Our opinions are a mix of biological and outside influences, so the essays include local facts about race, religion, topography, culture, GDP, and history.

The introductory essays are written to add context and hints on why common sense in a town of 12 people is crazy talk in a metro area of 18 million.

When I dreamed up the idea for the project, I was reading the posts of two-time Pulitzer winner Paul Salopek. He is on his own "slow journalism" project, walking around the world on a project called "Out of Eden Walk." I'm sure "slow journalism" and "slow bicycling" were associated in my dream.

When the day arrived for me to leave, my 16-year-old daughter, Grace, still harbored deep misgivings. She gave me the "you-might-not-make-it" hug.

"Don't worry, everything is going to turn out great," I said, just guessing myself.

I rolled the bicycle next to me, walking down the black asphalt driveway behind my home. With both hands holding onto the bicycle, I stepped on a tiny patch of imperceptible black ice.

My legs flipped out from under me. My feet flew high in the air, and I landed flat on my back. I thought people only fell like that in cartoons.

The bicycle fell on the side carrying the laptop and camera. It happened in a flash. I didn't get far, just ten feet away from my back gate.

All I planned or hoped to accomplish turned that single foot step. On an individual level, none of us really knows what's coming for us. We're all guessing. Sometimes life is as predictable as black ice moments and pandemics are full of them.

I collected myself and continued on my time-honored plan of hitting the road in search of understanding.

Buddha left his home to find enlightenment on his "noble search." Aristotle believed walking and talking unearthed the deepest philosophical truths. St. Paul was on the road to Damascus when he saw the light that saved his soul. Huck Finn and Jim journeyed down the Mississippi River.

The cyclist Albert Einstein believed in the power of the bicycle for insights into time and space.

"I thought of that while on my bicycle," Einstein said of the theory of relativity.

Einstein was probably riding slowly too.

Riding slow was part of it all. I never knew where I was spending the night because I never knew how far I was riding. I adopted a *Forrest Gump* credo.

"When I was tired. I slept," said Forrest Gump, in the 1994 movie. "When I was hungry. I ate. When I had to go, you know, I went."

I made a few informed editorial decisions people will object to but nobody will be confused. I chose to refer to the severe acute respiratory syndrome coronavirus and COVID-19 simply as Covid.

I also chose to beef up the length of selected quotes. They'll be much longer paragraphs than readers are familiar with reading. I wanted the exact rhythm, cadence and logic (or illogic) of the speaker to come across. *The Story Cycle* videos are unfiltered.

Lastly, I decided to reveal my observations at the conclusion of the book. Readers and I are on the same subjective journey.

My understanding of the pandemic changed me by the end of the ride and the challenge to readers is to be open to new insights too.

At the beginning of the ride, I was all questions. How close will my road stories be to those road stories told thousands of years ago? Might the pandemic stories of these days be similar to those told in the future?

A project born in a dream doesn't come fully formed. It develops with the miles. I was shocked when my pandemic questions turned into responses about life and death. People wanted to talk about what makes life worth living. Not just how to survive but why life is worth fighting for.

I was on a mission to listen, willing to be swept away by story worlds. I wanted to know what story junkies already know, that listening and learning might save lives. This challenge changed my life, and I hope it will change more lives.

Route 66 was the only choice for a symbolic, shared pandemic road. The Justinian and Antonine plagues raged down the 50,000 miles of roads built by the Roman Empire. The Black Death followed the Silk Road, killing 150 million people worldwide. Europeans brought their diseases to the Americas, wiping out 90 percent of the

Native Americans. After intermixing with *Homo sapiens*, Neanderthals may have gone extinct largely due to plagues.

The Covid pandemic has since crossed the one million mark for deaths in America and 15 million excess deaths around the world.

It's the most significant health crisis of our time. We need to learn from it and adapt to nature's seemingly eternal cycle of pandemics.

At the core of this Covid journey is a mystery. Why America has the highest Covid death toll on earth.

Beast of Main Street is about a slow rider on an ancient bicycle powered by curiosity. Along the way, people talk of meaning in their lives and the quest to make the most of life.

During a surge in deaths, in the depths of winter, bicycling slow along a road that's not really a road became a grand, life-affirming ride.

It's about our shared and flawed struggle to hang on to phantom life. It's a journey that promises to change the way you see this and future pandemics.

Let's ride.

"Then am I to understand that I have the smallpox?"
— **President Abraham Lincoln fell gravely ill after the Gettysburg Address. Lincoln likely infected his valet. William H. Johnson, 30, born the son of slaves, died of smallpox.**

.

"One guy said to me, ... 'Can we take you home. You've got a better chance at home. If we take you to the hospital, you may never come out.' And I said, 'Yes, you can take me home.'"
— **Walt Disney, a Chicago native and the founder of The Walt Disney Co. nearly died of the 1918 flu pandemic**

WORDS TO LIVE BY

ILLINOIS

*T*he traditional starting line of Route 66 is in front of the larger-than-life bronze lions guarding the Art Institute of Chicago. The north side lion is "on the prowl," and the south side lion is "defiant."

Both are ready to engage. Count me in.

What's the difference between Northside Cubs fans and a Southside Sox fans?

Cubs fans have never been south of the Art Institute. Sox fans have never been inside the Art Institute.

The ride begins in Chicago's showcase downtown. I rode through the snow and ice past Millennium Park, Grant Park, Buckingham Fountain, Shedd Aquarium, Adler Planetarium, Field Museum of Natural History, Soldier Field, McCormick Place, and the icy Burnham Harbor along the snowy bicycle path that rims the Lake Michigan shore.

The path veers into roads south along the lake past bungalows, parks, mom-and-pop shops, and factories with neighborhoods with concentrations of African Americans, Eastern Europeans, and Hispanics.

Turning west, I bicycled through Calumet City, Lancing,

Frankfort, Joliet, Manhattan, Elwood, Wilmington, Braidwood, Dwight, Pontiac, Lexington, Bloomington-Normal, Atlanta, Lincoln, Elkhart, Williamsville, Sherman, Springfield, Chatham, Divernon, Farmersville, Litchfield, Mount Olive, Worden, and Edwardsville on to the mighty Mississippi River.

By the time I made Joliet, there was no doubt about it, Route 66 is a theater of kitsch. It's both a functional local road and a roadside theme park.

Illinois is one of the top states for Route 66 memorabilia, with statues, fiberglass "muffler man" giants, murals, signs, restaurants, cafes, museums, billboards, and vintage motels. Route 66 shields are painted on the pavement and on small-town water towers. Old, abandoned gas stations are turned into Route 66 memorials.

Every state along the Route 66 corridor spreads the frosting on thick, and the frosting is vanilla white.

The real history of Route 66 is more diverse and shaded by the history of the nation. The Negro Motorist Green Book was developed in 1936 for African Americans traveling by car looking for barbers, beauticians, tailors, bars, stores, car repair shops, motels, and filling stations that wouldn't turn them away.

A "sundown town" was an all-White town or neighborhood that practiced racial discrimination. Black people needed to leave by sundown. All eight states along Route 66 had unofficial rules on race, and six had racist laws on the books, according to Candacy Taylor, "The Roots of Route 66," published in the *Atlantic*.

Much of the original Route 66 runs beside the old Chicago and Alton Railroad tracks, which were built on old Indian trails. These days, Interstate 55 runs next to farm and frontage roads now deemed Historic Route 66.

In the small cities, traffic was tight. In farm country, I moved to the side for combine harvesters.

I rode past isolated railroad crossings, snowy flat farmlands, weathered barns, white-painted farm homes, long rural driveways, and 16-story windmills. Not a scarecrow in sight.

History was my imaginary friend as I rode. I thought of the pre-

Columbian tall grass prairies and the Mississippian culture that built a lost city at the Cahokia Mounds.

I imagined once booming, lusty mining towns on the Illinois Coal Basin, which covers about 65 percent of the state. Illinois has 82 ghost towns, many of them former coal mining towns.

There were generations of families focused on their main streets, livelihoods, and churches. I imagined all the forgotten strife and affections.

Burma Shave limericks are a tradition on Route 66. Outside Dwight, I saw a series of signs evenly spaced saying, "Burma Shave/we till the land/we turn the soil/we use the ethanol/instead of oil."

On the other side of the happy, happy Route 66, I rode for miles along bleak 66. There were "Out of Business" signs on motels, furniture stores, and cafes. Boarded-up buildings sometimes outnumbered open businesses on small-town main streets. Rural America's dramatic income gap and rural blight must shade their opinions of the outside world.

It does matter where a person grew up and lives. It's the "nature" part of the nature vs. nurture debate. I expect kids from the southwest side of Chicago and downstate Atlanta to have different points of view.

Where we stand on the pandemic has much to do with where we live during a pandemic. Not just upstate or downstate but in which state of mind.

"I think things have changed for good now"

CRAIG THOMPSON DIDN'T LOOK like the typical bicycle rider.

No bike pants. No helmet. No bicycle gloves. All he needed was a hoody, a beat-up overcoat, and a pink cell phone in his top pocket.

We met while riding and he helped me navigate many of the side streets on Chicago's South Side. About 80 percent of the historic

Route 66 is still rideable, but my bicycle map steered me toward bicycle paths on the South Side.

Unfortunately, the unplowed bicycle paths were too snowy to ride, so Thompson and I improvised by riding along local roads.

He'd been "struggling for work" during the pandemic. Before the pandemic, he held some iconic Chicago jobs, from political worker to tour boat worker. They all ended with the lockdowns.

"I worked on the tour boats in Chicago, the architecture tours," he said. "I also worked sometimes on the replica canal boat in LaSalle-Peru. It's a replica of the canal boats. It's actually drawn by a mule. I was piloting that a few times. And during the winter times, I did telephone marketing for the Chicago Symphony Orchestra. And they ended their season because of Covid. I did do some political work. And I've done some house painting."

The pandemic gave him extra time he isn't sure what to do with.

"Mostly, I've just been riding my bicycle because I have nothing else to do," he said.

As for social distancing, he gives himself a "C+" or "B-".

"I've gone into bars a few times," he said. "Ya, I wear a mask if I hop on a train. I don't hop on trains that much. I did go with a friend to a family gathering in the Upper Peninsula of Michigan at Christmas time. I don't think there was ever any more than ten people there, and Covid was sort of non-existent in the county they were in."

Vaccines were not available to the general public at that point, but he was confident that he'd survive even if he got Covid.

"I think if I got it, I'd get through it, but I don't want to pass it to other people," he said.

He was frustrated by the lack of work and social isolation.

"I'm getting impatient with nothing going on, nothing to do, being bored all the time," he said. "I probably drink more than I should in the last year. And I'd like to have more of a social life than I've had in the last year."

Thompson believed that Covid and pandemics might be a permanent part of our shared future.

"I don't think this is a bump in the road, I think this is a turn in the road," he said. "I think things have changed for good now."

"Changed the way people are going to be"

GLENWOOD POLICE SGT. Zack Cotton flagged me down when he saw the "Tell Me a Story" sign on the back of my bicycle,

When he heard what I was doing, he was so enthusiastic about giving his opinions that I couldn't stop him.

He was a first responder in World War C, and touched on many heartfelt issues.

"I've dealt with it in my household," he said. "My wife tested positive for Covid just before Thanksgiving. I have two young kids, a four-year-old and a two-year-old ... When she tested positive, I had to stay home from work. Pull my four-year-old out of school. My wife got sick but not serious enough for hospitalization."

They struggled to get tested at the time because testing sites were overwhelmed. There was a three-day wait to get in, and an appointment was necessary. Results were taking seven to ten days.

"It was very frustrating for us," he said. "We were stuck at home. Obviously, through the Thanksgiving holidays, we had no one in our house. Couldn't see family."

The uncertainty made them anxious.

"I had to take some time off of work because I was exposed, but I didn't know if I was positive," he said. "It all worked out. My wife had no lasting effects from it."

Covid radically altered his work life too.

"As far as being a policeman, pretty much everything has changed," he said. "We have gone from making traffic stops and going and talking to people on calls to doing most of our stuff via the telephone. Medical calls, we don't go in the houses. We have to wear masks. We sanitize our cars. New policies and procedures come out all the time."

Police forces were among the first responders being vaccinated, and Cotton was vaccinated at the time of the interview in February.

"It has changed police work drastically for everybody," he said. "I don't know if things can ever go back to the way they were. We can only hope."

Cotton thought there'll be a before-Covid life and a living with Covid life.

"It has changed the way people are going to be, probably forever," he said. "It's changed the way people interact socially. I think it's changed people's habits ... the way people do things. What is considered normal personal space has changed. I don't think that is going to go back.

"I think more and more people are going to rely on the internet to do things that they may not have done before, including doctor's visits, shopping, getting prescription drugs, ordering food - I think a lot of those things are here to stay now."

His family missed "all the holidays," which is tough for a community-oriented family like his.

"We moved into a new house last year just before Covid started," he said. "One of the reasons we bought a new house is we wanted to entertain, and we haven't been able to do that. We normally throw some big parties at my house, you know, especially during the summer months. A pig roast. A crawfish boil. We haven't been able to do those things because of Covid."

An unexpected good side effect was more family time.

"I spend more time at home with my kids, just because there's nothing else to do," he said.

Boredom was a problem.

"I think it's really going to affect children," he said. "Their social skills are going to suffer. Their schoolwork is going to suffer. I think they're losing out on educational opportunities right now. And I think that's going to be lasting. I don't think we have even begun to see the lasting impacts of this."

As for his personal experience of happiness, he said he didn't feel overall less happy. Cotton became the first person of many on the trip who felt the same.

"I'm pretty resourceful," he said. "I find ways to entertain myself. Try to keep an upbeat attitude. Try to roll with the punches like everyone else."

"For me, I chose the irresponsible way"

MICHAEL SORENSON WAS between classes and coming out of Pugh Hall on the SIU campus in Normal when he agreed to talk about college life in pandemic times.

A Southern Illinois University senior majoring in secondary education, he expressed strong concerns for others and said alone time was giving him more time for self-reflection. A resident of Morton Grove, a Chicago suburb, he was also frank about his need for social interaction.

He'd already caught a mild case of Covid, so he didn't think he was going to get the first round of vaccines and would decide later what to do.

In the meantime, he had the antibodies to keep him safe for a few more months. He had strong doubts that masking or distancing were doing much good. Most people, he said, aren't masking properly or distancing during parties.

Maintaining one's mental health and social interactions, he said, are part of surviving the pandemic too.

"So I chose the irresponsible way," he said, "and I want to have fun with all my friends, especially when most of my friends are gone after this year. I think if we're all knowledgeable about it, we can stop it sooner rather than later and hopefully not be in another quarantine for another, approaching, a year."

He wasn't able to go to Bears games or play his senior year of college-level hockey. On the upside, he dropped "like 40 pounds" over quarantine.

"I found out a lot of cool stuff about myself," he said. "I found out I like being, I won't say being alone, but ... it gives you time to think."

He wasn't significantly more unhappy during his senior Covid year.

"Covid sucks," he said. "It probably sucks for a lot of people, but for me, it didn't do me that bad."

When it's all over, he said, "People will try to go out and have fun again."

"Sometimes I worry about my grandparents"

TWELVE-YEAR-OLD KOBIE BUNNER was standing across the street from the twenty-five-foot-tall Hot Dog Muffler Man, a fiberglass roadside tourist attraction in Atlanta.

He'd been playing around the town square, along old Route 66, the main street in town. I asked how life in a pandemic was going for him.

"It's been pretty good," he said. "Atlanta's a small town. They weren't too worried about it. But they still took their precautions and stuff to take care of the town. The park was closed and stuff, which was a little disappointing because a lot of kids like to hang out. But we still made that work."

He didn't know anyone who'd gotten sick. He'd been tested "like four times" at school and before family gatherings.

"Sometimes I worry about my grandparents, but everyone tells me I'm a kid and we shouldn't worry about it," he said. "Anyone can get Coronavirus, but the older you get, the higher risk you get."

Dances at school were canceled during the year. The IHSA recently began allowing sports but without fans in the stands.

He was in cheer, but that was canceled too. Of course they cancelled "cheer" in a pandemic.

People were adjusting, and Brunner looked forward to better days. Still, he wondered if things will ever be the same.

"We adjusted to it, and if it happens again, we know what it's like," he said. "It's not going to be perfectly normal, but it's better than nothing."

Teens Talk of Life & Death

THREE TEENAGERS WERE MESSING around on the town square across the street from the town's Route 66 roadside attraction, a 25-foot-tall Hot Dog Muffler Man statue.

Instead of a muffler, the Hot Dog Muffler Man holds a giant hot dog because the giant was once owned by a Cicero hotdog joint. From Atlanta to Los Angeles, giant fiberglass Paul Bunyans hold all sorts of things for local businesses. The giants were developed as roadside attractions in the 1960s.

In ancient times, a giant statue in the center of a village would be a god or a prophet. A hot dog god.

Route 66 is the main street of Atlanta, pop. 2,063.

From the start, I made the mistake of calling Atlanta a small town. It's all relative.

Sixteen-year-old Denver Atherton pointed out that Atlanta isn't that small for rural, agricultural Illinois. Down the road, Lawndale had a population of 144 people.

Neveah Linski, age 14, pointed out they have a Casey's gas station and a Dollar General nearby.

The pandemic changed their everyday lives and threw a scare into Steven Birdsell, age 14.

"I usually do wrestling, but I decided not to because of Covid," Birdsell said, who got Covid, along with his grandmother, mother, and sister. His grandmother had pre-existing conditions and suffered the most.

They were thinking about life and death more than teenagers in other generations, but they didn't feel that it changed them as people all that much.

"I didn't have any close relatives that have had Covid," Atherton said. "Me personally, and this is just my opinion, but I don't think Covid is what it's hyped up to be. For older people, yes, but for people 20 and under, it's not hardly a concern."

Vaccinated people maybe "shouldn't be required to wear a mask," Linski added.

Birdsell agreed but worried that family members may not be symptomatic but still infectious. Precautions, such as masks, should still be taken.

The kids weren't accustomed to being asked their opinions on anything, much less life and death in a pandemic.

Small towns, Linski said, have their own unique dynamics.

"I have my main group," she said. "so if one goes down, we're all going down."

On a scale of 1 to 10, 10 being the highest, Linski said the last year was a five-and-a-half.

"I don't see no difference. I still do the same stuff that I usually do," she said.

Atherton said the masks and Covid canceled "a lot of stuff for me, personally."

"In a small town here, it really isn't that big of a deal because there are (fewer) people," Atherton said. "This town doesn't really have to be as worried about Covid because it is a smaller town, and there aren't as many people who can get it. It's still required, but it isn't as big a deal as in bigger towns like it is in Chicago or a Bloomington or an L.A."

Birdsell talked after the interview to clear up what he said during the interview. He worried about his grandmother but felt awkward talking about it. He took some good-natured ribbing from his friends in the video.

Atherton turned the tables on me,. Why did I think it was important to ride a bicycle across the country asking pandemic questions.

If I was driving, I said, I'd probably have never stopped to talk to teenagers on a small town square.

Then he summarized his thoughts about his pandemic year in Atlanta.

"I just wish it would end, personally," he said.

"You don't know if there is a future"

RHONDA L. BROWN and Audra Von De Bur were co-workers standing outside sharing a smoke in Springfield.

Brown was from a nearby small town named Tovey, pop. 512. Both her brother-in-law and sister-in-law died of Covid the previous December. At the end, they were isolated and on ventilators. Their memorial service was virtual.

Both Brown and Von De Bur kept working all year for a remittance center. They'd seen the remittances business increase as more people sent more money home during the crisis.

Von De Bur had her first vaccination at the Illinois State Fair grounds and was waiting for her second shot.

"The downside for me is I haven't been able to see my friends for a year," she said as she teared up. "You know, we've all stayed away from each other. I haven't seen a lot of family. I had one uncle who was 75 years old and in the hospital with Covid, and he pulled through. I've been very fortunate for that. I haven't had anybody really close to me have it."

Von De Bur said she had "pre-existing" health conditions and was worried about catching Covid, "but we've been taking extreme precautions this year."

At the time, sanitizing chairs, countertops, and common areas was given more attention than the airborne spread of Covid.

Von De Bur said she arrived to work as early as 5 a.m., to sanitize the workplace for her fellow workers.

"It's kinda scary," Brown said, "it hits so close to home."

Nobody knows the best way to help each other, Von De Bur said.

"Mentally, it's tiring," Von De Bur said. "There's the constant worry for your family and your friends."

Brown couldn't see her grandchildren for three months.

"When you can't be around the people you love, it's taxing on you," Von De Bur said. "Rhonda and I are of an age where we're older, and we depend on a lot of get-togethers. A lot of it's been by text and FaceTime and trying to keep up a relationship with people that way."

Von De Bur said they cope by not letting it consume their thoughts.

"I appreciate work," Von De Bur said. "It's kept my mind off of things."

Von De Bur added that she gets out of Springfield to the rural farm areas to go fishing and relax in a small-town environment.

They both had no trouble ranking their pandemic life: "2019 was a 10 and 2020 was a 1."

"It's devastating," Von De Bur said. "This year, pretty much, was the bottom of the barrel for a lot of people."

As for the future, Von De Bur waxed philosophical.

"You don't know if there is a future," she said. "Our future is uncertain now because it will never be like the past again. They talk about the new normal, but it doesn't feel normal to us. But I don't see it going back to the way it was."

Asked for her final thoughts, Brown mentioned prayer.

"I pray to God, for the future," she said, "that we're still here."

After the interview, Von De Bur talked about people who lost their jobs to the pandemic. A tent city arose in Springfield. People donated sanitizers, soaps, and other supplies. The Salvation Army opened a warming center. The community worked to get people placed

The tent city eventually disbanded. But it was still winter, and displaced people were desperately seeking shelter.

"The homeless population doesn't have the means," she said. "They don't have any way to keep clean and sanitized against this virus. I don't know how many of them are in the (death toll) numbers."

She worried about the homeless. Were they getting vaccinated?

Where do they recover when they are sick? She was thinking of others.

She just wanted the homeless to "be able to live with it and stay healthy."

"It's been awesome for our marriage"

JEFF CAMPBELL DROVE in from Belleville to Springfield to put in an open bid for a government contract.

I found him waiting for his local contact near the Lincoln Home National Historic Site Visitor Center, which was closed due to the pandemic.

His pandemic story, Campbell said, was "kinda ironic" because he contracted the virus during the Thanksgiving holiday.

"Thanksgiving is my favorite holiday, so I couldn't taste nothing, drink nothing or anything like that," Campbell said. "It totally ruined my favorite holiday. It totally knocked me on my butt for about six days. I was exhausted."

At the time, people were under the impression that it primarily spread by touch, so he thought he might have contracted the virus from a keypad, a pen, or a door handle. His wife got Covid, too, but she just lost her taste.

"I figure everyone's going to get it," he said. "Which is ironic because I have a best friend who has been around it three times. And he's never gotten it. So it picks and chooses who it wants."

He had faith in his "pretty strong immune system" and never feared for his life. He felt like it was a strong flu.

One benefit of the isolation and working hybrid was his savings rate.

"I actually became real frugal with my money because all I could do is sit at home. I couldn't do nothing,. So I actually paid off a bunch of bills," he said. "I'll actually became debt free by May ... I took a negative and turned it into a positive."

The government response, he said, has been "as best they could."

"What do you do when you get hit in the face with something you've never seen or understood before?" he said. "I know there's a lot of finger-pointing and blaming. But what do you do when you are just learning about it as you're going along?"

The pandemic year didn't stress him out because he was focused on new developments in his personal life.

He married in November 2019 and came back from his honeymoon in Dublin, Ireland when Covid began taking hold. His wife was a teacher who began working from home with remote learning classes. He began working from home too.

"It's been awesome for our marriage," he said. "We've got to know each other and learn (about each other) ... We're stronger for it."

As for the future, he thought, it will be more of the same.

"This is our new flu. There are so many variants now, I think it's here to stay."

"It's do or die" in Farmersville

LOCAL FARMERS KNOW all about surviving through bad years, and it was a bad one for the only restaurant/bar in Farmersville.

Farmersville, pop. 724, is 25 miles south of Springfield along I-55 and Historic Route 66.

It was a Friday during the Lenten season, so the Caddyshack Sports Bar & Grill was gearing up for the ever-popular Friday night fish fry.

Owner Stephen Mainwaring sat down in a spare moment to talk about his special town, full of good, supportive people.

"It's been kinda tough all year being in the restaurant business," he said. "Trying to survive, ya know, and keep the doors open ... We've been here going on 11 years and fought through a lot. This has been a tough one."

He never closed the doors, but he switched to all carry-out for a time while he ran the place with his wife. Most of the staff came back after the Caddyshack returned to 50 percent capacity service.

"We have a good town that supports us. I think that's how we got through this," he said. "It's a town of 800, and it supports us very well."

The pandemic stress was worse because it threatened to take away his livelihood.

"It's do or die," he said. "You just have to do it to survive."

He was hopeful that the mask mandates might be lifted by June. He noted that Texas and Mississippi already got rid of their mask mandates.

Southern Illinois often feels like the South, but it's unmistakably Midwestern farm country around Farmersville.

Asked how the government handled the pandemic, he did not criticize.

"I can't say bad, I guess," he said. "It's a mass pandemic, you know, how do you do it all at once? You can't. It's our government, it's whatever you want to think of it. They're getting everyone vaccinated. I guess that's the most important part."

He laughed when asked if he spent more time at home with the family. Unfortunately, it was winter, so his main way of getting out of the house - golf - wasn't practical that time of year.

On a scale of 1 to 10, he rated his happiness level at about a 5.

"We survived, ya know, we put a tent up outside when it was nice out and had a lot of outdoor dining. So that helped us a lot too," he said. "Like I said, just fight and survive."

It all made him appreciate life a bit more.

"It makes you kinda appreciate what you got and how important your life is and your livelihood, you know," he said. "You feel fortunate being where you're at and doing what you're doing."

Off camera, he said some customers paid their dinner bill and followed up at the bar, leaving a private extra cash donation on the countertop.s

The farmers of Farmersville knew times will get better, and when they come, there'll be a good Friday night fish fry nearby.

"It ain't what you don't know that gets you into trouble. It's what you know for sure that just ain't so."
— Mark Twain, Missouri-born writer, cholera survivor

"It looks like the coronavirus is being weaponized as yet another element to bring down Donald Trump ... The coronavirus is the common cold, folks."
— Rush Limbaugh, the late Missouri-born conservative radio host

ANGELS OF THE OZARKS

MISSOURI

*S*omebody save me. The weather was typical of March in Missouri, blowing rainstorms, freezing nights, frosty mornings, and tornados.

I crossed the steel truss McKinley Bridge over the Mississippi River into a northern industrial section of St. Louis before lying down dead asleep under the Gateway Arch.

After a bit of sightseeing and a few interviews, night was falling and I was frantically seeking a place to pitch my tent for some stealth camping. Maybe in a grove of trees, a forest preserve or a cemetery. But not a tombstone in sight.

After a chance meeting, a former college history professor put me up for the night. His hobby was giving history tours of cemeteries.

The next night, I was riding into Sullivan when I spotted a cemetery dating back to the Civil War hidden in a grove of trees. I pitched my purple tent in the graveyard, crawled inside, closed my eyes, and disappeared.

Two-thirds of the people in the Civil War died of "major infectious diseases of the era." More than 450,000 deaths were due to the so-called Third Army of disease. Humans killing humans by mere proximity. On each side, the enemy was us.

Then it came to me that the war had a long tail, like Covid will. I wondered if the wrong lessons are being learned or if the wounds will go on and on in ways no one quite yet knows.

Just outside of Rolla, I came across a washed-out bridge and was forced to backtrack. I rode a 144-mile detour loop along US Route 63 to US Route 60 before rejoining Route 66 in Springfield.

Outside of Springfield, a long-brewing storm finally let loose. The rain was horizontal. Lightning and thunderclaps shook the air. Tornados touched down in the next county. On cue, my wobbly rear tire went flat.

I pulled off a few feet from the road onto a muddy, gravely shoulder to make repairs. Cars and trucks splashed by. Their backdraft pulled me backward.

Suddenly, out of the storm drove a white Ford pickup truck. When the window rolled down, I saw an older Ozark man. He was silent at first.

"Kind of a bad day for a bike ride, isn't it?" he said in a slow rural drawl.

Sensing that he was offering a ride, I said no thanks. I wasn't hitchhiking Route 66.

"Well, it's five o'clock," he said, "and you're not going to get to Carthage before sundown."

More wind and rain.

"The tent will become a kite," he said, "with the wind the way it is."

Long pause. More traffic. More misery.

"It's 15 miles to Carthage," he said, "and I can get you there in 15 minutes."

"Sometimes," I said, "it takes people the longest time to understand the simplest truths. Thank you!"

I threw the bicycle in the truck bed and hopped into the cab. Ritchie was a retired granite worker and asked if his wife could come along for the ride. We drove back to their house to pick her up. I wonder what she thought of me.

The three of us drove to Carthage, and I checked into a motel. I spent the night fixing the tire.

The following morning, I realized the rear wheel was not salvageable and prepared to walk the 15 miles to the next bicycle shop.

"Need some help?" yelled a grey-bearded man from the front door of the nearby Bud's Bait shop.

I learned my lesson during the storm - accept help when it's offered.

"Can you help?" I shouted back.

Bait shop manager Sam "Stinger" Stanley was a Covid long-hauler. I'm convinced he'd have fixed the bicycle himself if he could, with the gear in the bait shop.

Instead, he convinced a shop customer to give me a ride to the front door of the nearest bicycle shop in Webb City.

Specialized Bicycles owner Debbie Johnson put my bicycle at the front of the line. She later gave me a tour of Joplin, which suffered a devastating tornado a decade earlier.

She told harrowing stories and pointed out where real angels were once seen helping tornado victims.

Once the angels did their good deeds, they mysteriously disappeared. Not people helping people. Angels helping people. To some around Joplin, the angels are folk stories. To others, angels are fact.

I, too, was swooped up to safety when I needed it most in Missouri. There were thousands of kindnesses, too many to relate. I was meeting angels of the human variety on Route 66.

The Laughing Panhandler

Joseph William Bonnett laughed while talking about the good old days before the pandemic. Pandemic times were lean times for a panhandler.

African American and homeless, he asked me for a dollar on 13th Street and Washington Avenue. I bribed him for the interview.

He did not mention using the pandemic times as a new opportunity to get off the streets. He just wanted his old life back.

"The Coronavirus has affected me a lot in St. Louis because there are less people walking around," he said. "So it's harder to make money ... It's harder to panhandle for food. The shelters are more stricter. The businesses are more stricter. The McDonald's lobby has been closed almost for a year now. Walgreen's hasn't been walkable. There have been a lot of places that has been closed.

"If you're homeless and you deal with the public more, it's less people you can grab and talk to. And get help from," he said. "So it just makes the wait longer and more frustrating because everybody's dealing with the virus now."

He was afraid of the virus, but he didn't know anybody with it. He contracted flus all his life. He'd been testing for Covid at the homeless shelter, but it sounded like he was reluctant to get the shot. At the time, the vaccine was not widely available for the homeless.

I asked him if he was more afraid of death than in the past, but he seemed to dismiss my "death question" as a passing thought.

"I have been more afraid of death," he said. "I've never seen the academics like this. I mean, the library's been closed. Schools been closed."

At the start of the pandemic, he said, it was interesting to see so few people out on the streets. But wasn't "as funny anymore because I'm seeing less and less people. It gives a strange vibe."

I asked if he felt any anxiety about the pandemic.

"I have a little anxiety," he said. "But I'm just waiting for people to open their businesses back up. I'm ready to be getting back to eating in lobbies of fast-food restaurants and getting found drinks and stuff like that."

Then he flashed a wide smile and laughed hard.

"I'm not taking a shot. I haven't been sick"

JESSICA AND EFFEREM JOHNSON were healthy, happy, and looking for a Sunday brunch along Washington Street when I met them.

They didn't know anyone with Covid. They were more afraid of the vaccine than getting Covid, so they did not intend to vaccinate. They didn't know of many people in their African American community who had been vaccinated yet.

Testing was mandated for Efferem Johnson, who worked in "transportation" in St. Louis, but he was "on the fence" about getting a shot.

"As far as I'm concerned," he said, "I don't believe these numbers. Covid, Covid, Covid, Covid, Covid, Covid. These numbers. These numbers. These numbers. But in actuality, we haven't seen anything."

Because he didn't know anyone with Covid, Efferem said, "there's no reason to get the shot."

Jessica felt the same. She hadn't seen anyone sick, so there was no reason to get the vaccine or to be tested.

"I know I'm not taking a shot," she said. "I haven't been sick. Nobody around me has been sick."

Jessica was forced to quit her job to babysit their preschooler and parent their other child who was taking remote classes. She started up a new candle business on her own, and it was doing well. But the pandemic was taking "a toll on her."

"It was extremely hard being home all the time," she admitted.

Going to work with the transportation department made it easier on him, Efferem said, because it kept him out of the house.

They are getting more family time together but their waistlines suffered, Efferem laughed.

Jessica called the pandemic "just a mess" and wanted it to be "over."

They agreed that they couldn't wait to stop wearing masks and get back to normal. Efferem mentioned that Texas and Arizona already got rid of their mask mandates, and "we're hoping that (the loosening of restrictions and mask mandates) is coming this way."

"We're ready to get back to our normal lives," Efferem said.

When the camera went off, Efferem cautioned me to get out of downtown before dark, it wasn't safe. The pandemic wasn't keeping the criminals at home.

Defense Contractor Changed how He Works

A VETERAN and Scott Air Force Base support contractor, Matthew S. Miller saw a national security side of the pandemic.

When I corralled them, Miller and his wife were strolling down Washington Avenue in search of a brunch. They lived across the Mississippi River in Illinois at Scott Air Force Base, in Bellville, Illinois.

"Overall, I've had about 20 percent of my personnel come down with it in one form or fashion," he said. "And in the summer, my customers, as well, came down with Covid, which caused us all to go into tracing all that sort of thing ... we had 25 to 30 people or somewhere around there that came down it at some point."

There were times, he said, he didn't know who was healthy and who was sick.

He was saving money, ditching the commute, and living free of the dreaded workplace cubicle.

"I'm saving the hassles," he said. "The dry cleaners. The packing the lunches. All the things you have to do when you stay in the cubicle all day long. So like, the school bell would ring to start work, and the school bell would ring for everyone to leave at four thirty or five o'clock. That is gone. So that's a good thing. That's a real blessing, I think. I really enjoy the fact now that you go into your job and leave."

Knowing what to do during the year also caused some family friction between his elderly parents and his sister in South Dakota, where restrictions were more lax.

"My mom and my dad are about 80," he said. "And they have some massive anxiety over this. Whenever I talk to them, they're very nervous about going anywhere. Whereas my sister and brother-in-law live in Dakota, and they're just polar opposites. So it is kind of interesting. And when they go to see each other, they are arguing about wearing masks. So that's been an interesting development."

He wasn't sure, but he thought he and his wife might have had a mild case. Miller's wife (who declined an interview) worked at the local YMCA and was around many people.

As for their marriage, he looked at her as he said, "we survive through this, we can survive through most anything."

"I'm fairly certain that we have run across it and just kind of muddled through it," he said. "I am pretty sure we both have had it."

He was vaccine hesitant but realized vaccination might become a prerequisite for his defense job.

"I'd like to get that Johnson & Johnson (vaccine), one and done," he said. "And be done with it. But I'm not going to fight it. But I'm not out there looking for it either. I'm not that worried about it. I have good health, but if they come around and say come get it - and I don't have to stand around for a long time or sit there in the queue - I'll go get it, yes."

History teaches us, he said, that Americans will probably forget how they felt and how they worked during the pandemic.

"It's been an experiment," he said. "And I'm hoping that we do remember some of these functions and how they happened and the lessons learned. But I'm not going to hold out a lot of hope for that. I think that things have changed so often, and we don't ever remember what happened yesterday and just keep on relearning these issues."

Pandemic through the Lens of Family History

NIGHTFALL WAS COMING, and Harold Karabell was riding his bicycle in the opposite direction when he yelled to me, "Where are you headed?"

"I'm going to L.A."

We talked a bit, and I boldly asked if he had "a nice warm shower."

Friendly, generous, and in my age range, Karabell pulled out his cell phone and called his wife Karen to see if she'd agree. I spent the night in their guest house behind their home. I luxuriated in the warm shower and raided their full refrigerator. Harold Karabell even agreed to be interviewed in the morning.

A native of Indianapolis, Karabell was a University of Indiana history professor before moving to St. Louis 36 years previous to run a property management firm specializing in historic properties.

People who died in his network of friends, but nobody in his immediate family "has exhibited serious symptoms."

He tried to keep the pandemic in perspective by coming at it from an intellectual point of view.

"We have a number of tenants," he said. "As you might expect, quite a few have been affected one way or the other by the novel coronavirus."

Some of his tenants worked at restaurants and in the tourist and hospitality industry. When their industry went into a depression, "a number of these people don't have much in the way of financial resources to fall back upon."

"They lost their jobs, and we've had to scramble to find ways to get them rental assistance and to work out all sorts of payment plans," he said. "We're very understanding with people, given the fact that we have enormous bills to pay as well just to keep the business and the buildings operating."

Short-term rentals are another part of his real estate business, similar to Airbnb. That part of his business "tanked."

"That part of the market has somewhat recovered," he said, "but for a while, we were in desperate financial straits."

Asked if the pandemic and his financial woes caused him anxiety, he digressed to tell a story from his personal history.

His mother was just ten years old when the 1918 pandemic first arrived in America.

"She remembered seeing body after body being taken out of neighboring houses and apartment buildings," he said. "So I've lived my entire life with that knowledge ... that a pandemic is not necessarily a thing of the past."

His anxiety was that he might live to see a hemorrhagic virus like Ebola, with an even higher death toll. He expected a pandemic but was shocked by the "lack of preparedness" by the government.

His family was limiting their gatherings to immediate family. He was masked during our entire interview.

One of the positive "byproducts" of the pandemic, he said, was that the variety and quality of home cooking took off.

"It's great to rediscover the joys of eating at home," he said, adding that he once was an avid restaurant-goer. "My wife, Karen, who was a great vegetarian cook before the pandemic, has become a gourmet vegetarian cook."

Another byproduct has been an appreciation for life.

"I hope that all of us," he said, "have learned to take absolutely nothing for granted."

For instance, he said, St. Louis escaped the polar vortex that pulverized the Midwest from Chicago to Texas. I left on the Route 66 bicycle ride from Chicago days after it moved east.

"One should learn," he said, "to appreciate the blessings of life even more because of the pandemic and things like the polar vortex."

As for rating his happiness on a scale of 1 to 10, he essentially said life's too complicated for that.

"I don't expect life to be easy," he said. "I've never had a high happiness level."

He thought masking and distancing were going to be a fact of life "until we approach something like herd immunity and until the overwhelming number of us are vaccinated."

"The good old days were never the good old days," he said, remembering his mother, who also survived diphtheria.

When Karabell's son was 10-years-old, he caught his grandmother lamenting the state of modern times.

"Grandma," his son said, "remember when you were a younger woman? The Holocaust was a great old time, wasn't it?"

He ended the interview by recalling our chance meeting while riding bicycles in opposite directions in St. Louis.

"It was completely serendipitous," he said. "If you're a person of faith, you can call it providential just to meet you going opposite directions on my bicycle, being intrigued by your load and your sign on the back. And turning around and talking to you. And I'm glad it's worked out so beautifully. So call it serendipitous, fortuitous, providential, I'm glad it worked out for everyone."

Before I rode away, he handed me a one dollar bill. The former history professor knew symbolic gestures are communication on another level. I took it as a wish for luck on the way.

The message came in loud and clear and was remarkable for another reason. It wasn't the last similar gesture along Route 66. It came in the form of a prayer circle around the Pequod. A polished rock to hang around my neck. Free homemade cookies and a blessing for the road.

Who knows if we can really carry mere wishes for protection but I caught the meaning.

Cashier with an MBA Tells a Cliffhanger

WHEN LINDA TREVINO CROTHERS heard I was outside her Dollar Tree store interviewing people about the pandemic, so she stopped working at the cash register and ran outside to tell a real-life cliffhanger.

I was at the Ellisville Dollar Tree asking exiting customers for an interview. I was seeking a diversity of interviewees and hadn't yet landed an interview with a retail person working through the pandemic while others were working and isolating at home.

Covid put Crothers behind the counter at the dollar store. She was the holder of advanced engineering degrees and an MBA from Purdue University. She stood in front of the plastic flower display, telling her life's journey from project engineer to cashier.

The Texas native was once a senior project engineering manager working with Indiana Bell, Time-Warner, Verizon, and then AT&T in Arizona, California, Florida, Texas, and the Midwest.

When the pandemic struck, she went to 100 percent remote work until business dropped off and her contract expired.

"It was great to be home with my daughter. She's disabled. So she's home all day," she said. "And I have a bunch of golden retrievers."

Hard times coincided with the pandemic's arrival.

"We were first impacted in late February when my son's Boy Scout (leader) was ill ... Finally, they admitted him to the hospital, and two days later, he died," she said. "That was a big wake-up call for me on how serious this was."

Her son became anxious about going out anywhere in public and eating out. She and her husband masked up and began socially distancing.

Then several elderly cousins died. Her disabled, elderly mother and sister were sick for weeks. Her nephew was sick for six weeks. A family wedding turned into a super-spreader when 70 people gathered for the event.

"My entire family was pretty scared about Covid," she said. "My whole family has been drastically impacted."

She lost her senior project manager job almost ten months previous to our interview. During that year, she worked consulting, robotics, furniture sales, and at Dollar Tree. Her husband was a school construction worker but lost his job when schools shut down.

Her family was near a financial collapse. They were struggling to pay the rent. Her daughter dropped out of her freshman year of college. The longer Crothers stayed unemployed in the engineering field, the more outdated her skills were getting.

They weren't bankrupt or homeless. But they were in dire straits and toughing it out. Life wasn't safe and sound. The clock was ticking on her value in the marketplace she wanted to work. They were living on the edge.

The walls were closing in.

"I have been impacted greatly," she said. "I have days when I am just dragging. It's very difficult for me. I get very depressed. I have high anxiety. Financial stresses. Trying to make the rent payment. Trying to ensure that life is kinda seamless for my children."

She sought help for depression.

"I have a doctor who gives me prescribed medication," she said. "I don't know how well I'd be able to manage all this without the assistance of the medication. I know sleep, diet, and exercise all play a big role, but it gets to a point where it's just overwhelming."

As for final observations, she was a fan of the post-apocalyptic TV horror show, *The Walking Dead*.

"I feel like this was a little taste of the apocalypse coming, just a dash of it," she laughed.

In the meantime, her husband recently found work as a bricklayer. Her daughter intends to go back to college in the fall or go online. Crothers loves being outdoors and talking to people to keep upbeat.

"I think it's a life lesson," she said. "It's hard for me to do my advice - but to focus on the now and the today. I have my long-term plans. But to be ready because (life) is going to be upset. Just kinda take a deep breath and say, 'This too will pass.'"

Her life was teetering on edge. Will she find peace and financial security? Will her big family survive intact? Will she ever work again as an engineer?

Life was already fragile and now a real-life cliffhanger.

Mother Watches Child Falling Behind

PATRICIA NOBLIN WAS her smoke break outside the Dollar Tree in Ellisville, an outer-ring suburb of St. Louis.

She and her co-workers that morning were talking about the pandemic, asking themselves if it was really so bad.

"We were discussing today the impact that Covid has had on us and how it hadn't impacted anybody," she said. "We've worked through the whole pandemic, and not one person that we have known ... contracted Covid."

The more she kept talking, however, the more she talked about remote schooling, her husband's temporary layoff, in-store restrictions, and the economic stimulus package.

"It's impacted businesses," she said. "We've seen less and less people coming into stores, doing a lot more online shopping and curbside pick-ups, and stuff."

Her husband was laid off for months when the local General Motors plant shut down.

"We were able to get that unemployment stimulus. That helped us out a lot," she said. "But no (huge) financial burden."

Her husband was back at work by then, and she was on the vaccine waiting list with the St. Charles County Health Department. Family gatherings dropped off, but she was looking forward to the pandemic ending.

"I hope and feel (the pandemic) is coming to an end," she said, "because we need to return to some kind of normalcy."

After turning off the camera, she added that the greatest impact was on her children's schooling. So I turned the camera back on.

Her youngest daughter was struggling at "below grade level."

"In the beginning, when we went to virtual learning, it did impact my children," she said. "I watched them struggle through it. There wasn't much guidance on the curriculum and what needed to be done. It has impacted them (when) they started back this year.

"My youngest one is, actually, below grade level. So it has impacted her in the fact that she wasn't able to be in school and in-school learning. Because they were very lax in the school district where I was at when it came down to virtual learning, very lax."

Her children slipped behind in school and are struggling to catch up.

"They are actually back now this year, and everything seems to be going a lot better," she said. "They are happier. They enjoy going to school. They enjoy learning."

A Pandemic App & Listening Jesus

BILL AND TERRI MENCHAK were out for a walk around their Ellisville neighborhood as I slowly rode by. The "Tell Me a Story" sign on the back of the bicycle sparked a conversation.

The Menchaks wanted to share their faith-based opinions. Later, they weren't going to let me go riding to Los Angeles without a touch of prayer power.

Bill Menchak was the president of Christian Cycling, a faith-based ministry of bicycle riders "who love Jesus."

"We use the bicycle as our vessel to tell people the good news of Jesus Christ," he said.

Pre-pandemic, there'd be different rides every night with different groups on road bicycles and mountain bikes. All that was curtailed with the onset of the pandemic.

"Due to the fear of Covid, it's kinda dwindled down. The numbers have decreased. A lot of people, including myself, have kinda avoided big mass-start rides," he said. "We'll ride with one or two friends, and we do a lot of stuff on an application called Zwift."

The bicycle virtual training application Zwift allowed him to ride a stationary bicycle in his office with his friends - in a virtual formation - around him as they rode through geographical settings around the world.

Bill Menchak was semi-retired, and Terri started working from home long before the pandemic.

"With Bill home from retirement, that was our big adjustment," she said. "Covid kinda didn't really play into it, except for the fact that he wasn't going outdoors quite as much. It's kinda fun because he's home all the time."

As for pandemic-related anxiety, Bill Menchak said he was finding retirement relaxing.

"The anxiety is gone," he said. "I'm not getting up and going to work anymore. I don't set an alarm clock. One of my favorite sayings is I got six Saturdays and one Sunday every week."

Terri was anxious about her 100-year-old neighbor, who was

quarantined in a nursing home. Terri hasn't been able to visit or care for her for more than a year.

"Because she has dementia, you can't Zoom with her," she said. "She's never seen a computer. She doesn't understand it. You also can't go visit her outside the window of the nursing home because then she thinks they are holding her prisoner. And she gets all upset because she wants to go with her friends and go out. So that's been really hard. So we hope they're going to make an exception for us. And actually let us go in. And have a party for her when she turns 100."

Terri intended to get a vaccine when it's available to her. Bill wasn't sure if he will get a vaccine.

"I'll wait to see if people grow a third eye," he said. "On such short testing, I'm skeptical is all, a little bit."

Both sides of their family contracted Covid. Terri Menchak's 86-year-old uncle was put on a respirator, "but it was his own fault because he refused to go to the doctor" until the Covid was advanced.

Overall, they were critical of the news media "over-sensationalizing" and "the money (the government) has spent on it."

"I'm hoping it's not just a social experiment to see how they can control the nation," he said. "I have no proof of that, just skeptical is all."

Terri Menchak said her thoughts went out to the kids.

"We hear that from our daughter, that the kids at the high school level," she said, "those kids are really struggling."

Bill Menchak reiterated his fears for the economy.

"I really empathize with the small business owners. The people who the government shut down, your restaurants and small businesses. Yet your Walmarts and Home Depots are all open."

When the interview ended, Bill said a prayer over me and the Pequod.

Both he and Terri bowed their heads

"Lord, we know you didn't send this," he said, and please keep this rider safe on his journey.

Then he thanked Jesus for "listening."

"It's all about protecting the ones that we love"

THE ST. James Public Library was closed due to the pandemic when I arrived in early March, but a cheery librarian, Sara Ray, came out to share her pandemic year.

None of her immediate family members were seriously ill yet, and nobody at the library had tested positive either.

"There are only three employees, so if one of us goes down, the rest of us are going down, as far as quarantine," she said. "And then we have nobody to replace us after that."

Her family gatherings were curtailed. Her friendship "bubble" was careful to mask up and socially distance. All her get-togethers were outside and distanced.

"It does get to you a little bit after a while because you just want it to be over," she said. "And my sympathy goes out to the people who have had it or have lost family members or friends. So I feel that through other people I know who have had others who passed away from it. That can be a little hard sometimes."

On a scale of 1 to 10, with 10 being the best, she rated the year of the pandemic a five or a six.

"It's been about medium," she said. "But I get it, because it's all about protecting ones that we love. And not ... spreading anything back and forth. So I will give that up for a year, until we are all out of this and can celebrate next year."

Covid Inspires Religious Zeal

EDUARDO DANIEL GUEVARA was cleaning my room at the Econo Lodge in Rolla when I met him.

In the heart of the Bible Belt and the Ozark Mountains, he was a working-class preacher in cleaning clothes.

He contracted Covid earlier in the year and was sweating it out in bed at home when he underwent a life-changing religious reawakening.

"I grew up in the church, but I strayed away, so far away, from our Lord Jesus Christ that he's opened me up, my eyes and my heart to knowing what's really important," he said. "Covid, actually, was a big thing that I went through that helped me a lot to reflect a lot on what I needed to do with my life."

In his pre-Covid life, he let depression and anxiety get to him, but that was spirited away during his quarantine.

His room was pitch black. His energy drained. Yet he found a renewed mission in life.

"I was going through a very weird phase in my life," he said. "I really didn't really know what I wanted to do."

His brother and sister also contracted Covid, and he gave them faith-based advice on how to handle it. Both took his advice, recovered, and landed better jobs when they got well. He credited divine intervention.

"God has blessed them."

He described what his "conversation with God" sounded like.

"He says, 'Alright, are you ready to try my way now? 'Cause I think you might like it. I think you'll be able to compare your old self to your new self.'"

Guevara was on a mission.

"I'm definitely in love with my new self," he said. "I recently started ... about a month and a half into my journey."

Simultaneously, he believed Covid was part of a larger Communist "conspiracy." The conspiracy was a shared conspiracy between the news, the media, and the government. He was certain that it is part of mind-control conditioning.

"I feel the Lord has lifted the veil to see what's in front of me, to really see what's going on," he said. "Logically, Covid does not make sense ... We're all like robots. They say do this. And we're like 'alright!' Without really doing our own research. Without looking further into it."

If boosters become necessary, that will be proof of the plot. As more proof, he points to restaurant masking policies making no sense because patrons take the masks off to eat. Why, he asked, because masking wasn't making people safer.

Vaccine shots, he believed, are part of the conspiracy, and he'll never get one.

"My belief about Covid is they are using it as a brainwash system," he said. "They want to get rid of the God gene, which is inside. We all have a third eye, which is the pineal gland ... All we can do is pray."

He thought America has lost its way.

"Even if you do have Covid," he said. "Even if you've lost a family member, I will assume that the family member that you have lost is in a better place. And the Bible says they will later come on the last day and reign with us here on earth with Jesus Christ.

"And ya ... just pray."

Of Hope and Havoc

MANAGER VICKI LEWIS saw an advancing Covid storm from behind the Econo Lodge front desk.

The hotel was cutting shifts and laying off workers. She was taking care of her daughter's children and their emotional crises. She can't lose this job. Not now.

"It's wreaked havoc with the hotel all year long," she said, "and it doesn't look like it's going to be letting up anytime soon."

Lewis knew Covid sufferers, and she worried about her 84-year-old father. She feared her exposure to the public at the motel front desk might kill him.

"For the longest time, when I'd go get his groceries or get whatever he needed, I would stand outside and talk to him," she said. "I was afraid to go in and talk to him."

At the same time, she was taking care of her grandchildren, 15 and 16 years old. After remote learning for an entire year, they were going back to school that week. It was a challenging year for the kids. She and her granddaughter were in counseling.

"Especially my granddaughter, it has affected her mental health a lot," she said. "She gets depressed. My grandson, it affects him, too, but he goes to his music and plays his music a lot. But they miss their friends and everything."

She worries about everyone around her.

"I feel l am under a lot more stress than I was," she said. "I stress about the guests not coming into the hotel. I worry about my grandkids. I worry about my dad. I worry about my husband. My husband is a truck driver."

Her husband was having trouble finding food on the road because places were shut down. So he equipped his truck with a refrigerator and cooking items.

"I'm hoping it's over with soon," she said. "And that things get better. So that everybody is able to go back to being the way they were. Being normal. Whatever that will be. Ya know?

"Everybody can go back to having picnics and going over to their family's houses for holidays. I mean, that's what's really hard. It's the holidays. Sitting at the kitchen table. That used to be filled all the way around with people that are no longer there with you."

"I'm Not Going to Get It"

MEGAN HODGES WAS cheerful as she talked about politics and the pandemic hoax.

Casually smoking her cigarette outside the Rolla Walmart, Hodges said the pandemic was not significant in her everyday life.

"None of us has gotten it," she said. "And none of us wear masks at all. Because we just don't see the point of it. I mean, it's been around for a year or so now ... There's the flu, and everybody gets the flu, and they're okay."

She was confident that she and her family will remain free of the virus until it dies down or goes away.

Her husband worked at FedEx delivering packages, and he didn't wear a mask. He worked maskless in the warehouse and delivered to homes.

"And Covid is supposed to live on boxes for 24 hours, and he has not caught it," she said, repeating a misconception from earlier in the pandemic.

Walmart shoppers were required to wear a mask, but she had just finished shopping maskless.

Her job at the local Hampton Inn asked that she wear a mask, and she refused. Her managers didn't enforce the rule.

"I haven't changed anything because I know I'm not going to get it, I mean, I haven't gotten it yet, and it's been over a year."

The reaction to the pandemic "might" be part political and part hoax.

"I feel like it was a little political," she said, adding it started about the beginning of the election year. "It seems really odd to me."

The "coincidence" of the pandemic coming in an election year was an election issue raised by President Trump.

Pressed to say if the pandemic was a hoax, she said, "I think so."

"I know a million people who don't wear masks and don't social distance, and they don't have it," she said. "I mean, look around. Everybody is not wearing a mask."

As for the future, she was confident that she and her family will not be devastated by the pandemic.

Yet the pandemic is real, she acknowledged. But the running national death toll is all "political."

She felt her life was normal during the pandemic.

She ended on a positive note.

"I just wish the crud would go away," she said. "It will eventually."

"Most people around here aren't too concerned"

As THE OWNER of a liquor store in the Ozarks, Jennifer Lavely meets a wide variety of people and most people didn't seem fazed by the pandemic.

"Seems like most people around here aren't too concerned about it," said Lavely, of mask-wearing compliance in the town of about 2,705 people.

Together with her husband, the Lavelys ran Route 63 Liquor in Licking, a converted gas station. They both were vaccinated as soon as possible and on the same day. Both experienced painful reactions. She suffered an aching stomach and high fevers.

"By the time I got home, my back was killing me, I was feeling really bad, so I took my temperature, and it was 101.8," she said. "I was just freezing, so I just reclined in the chair at home and just kinda sat there the rest of the night. My husband came home ... and had the same exact symptoms as I did, almost the exact same time. I woke up this morning and I felt fine."

Her brother and sister-in-law caught Covid but were not hospitalized. A few customers got it and died.

Not much around Licking changed in the last year, she said. Social gatherings were about the same. Liquor sales didn't rise or fall.

"It seems like more out-of-towner people come in here. It seems like they're the ones wearing masks," she said. "Most people around here do not. So, I don't know, it seems like most people around here aren't too concerned about it."

Despite the number of dead nationally and a few locally, she wasn't dealing with the pandemic in her everyday life.

She said she got vaccinated for others.

"I suppose we didn't have to get it," she said, "but we did."

Nevertheless, she was hoping for an end to the pandemic by the summer.

"I'm hoping the vaccine will help," she said. "I think the more people get it (the shot), the better. Definitely."

"I'm More Socially Anxious"

THE PANDEMIC ROCKED the normal high school and college milestones in Samantha Lavely's life.

High school graduation was delayed. Her prom was canceled. She was a freshman communications major at Truman State University but found communicating difficult.

"It's not what I expected," said Lavely, of Licking. "It's harder making friends. And talking to people. Talking to people in class because you have to be so far away from everybody. Most of it is just online for me now. I don't really get to talk to a lot of people."

She wasn't happy about any of it.

"It's definitely harder talking to people now, and I feel like, since the pandemic, I'm more socially anxious when it comes to trying to talk to people because I'm just not used to it anymore."

She was already vaccinated. She went to the front of the vaccination line despite preference given to people with underlying conditions. The local dispensary had extra vaccine shots on hand due to low demand in the area.

"I was able to get it," she said, "which I'm pretty thankful for."

Friendships were harder to maintain because some people moved away after high school. Making friends at her new college was tough, given distancing and masks.

"Hopefully, everybody will get the vaccine, and this will be ... diminished by August," she said.

All, she hoped, will be better by fall.

A Slug of Courage not Enough to Talk of Her

"I SUPPOSE he thought he'd break down if he mentioned her," said the owner of Route 63 Liquors.

Robert D. Clouse finished buying beer and a small bottle of whiskey before starting the interview at Route 63 Liquors in Licking.

He opened the whiskey bottle inside the store before the interview began. Took a hard swig and prepared himself.

Clouse didn't mention his wife, who recently died of Covid. Instead, he kept drinking and kept his heartbreak a secret.

He and the family were barred from visiting her when she was sick. She died in the hospital room alone. He was taking her death hard.

Sometimes, he broke into tears at the counter paying for his whiskey and beer.

When I asked him if anyone he knows contracted Covid or died, he mentioned people but not her. He was Covid-free, but his brother-in-law was hospitalized.

"I never got it," he said. "I have underlying conditions. I just stayed away when (others) had it."

His family was vaccinated, but "I don't know where to get it."

He had emphysema and intended to get a shot when he figures out where to go. But he's not worried about contracting Covid.

"I don't care. If I get it, I get it. If I don't, I don't," he said. "It's the luck of the draw, I guess."

As he spoke, he checked his jacket pockets.

"I have a mask, but I'll worry about that later," he said. "Nobody around here wears one anyway."

Nobody at the local restaurants and bars wears a mask, he said. The waitresses wore masks at one time but didn't anymore.

"We'll all get together on birthdays, holidays, that sort of thing," he said. "No masks. I guess it isn't as prevalent as it is in other cities right now."

He expressed empathy for the sick and those who have died, again not mentioning her.

"I feel sorry for the people who have passed," he said. "And there's probably going to be a lot more. I think now that the government got rid of stupid-ass Trump, I think they're going to be doing pretty good with the vaccination stuff."

He hoped the vaccine would end the pandemic.

"I think it's going to come to an end once everyone starts getting vaccinated," he said. "Then I think everything will be okay."

He "quarantined" and "wore the mask outside" when asked during the year. But he worried for the health of other people.

"You just gotta do what you gotta do," he said. "Do your part to help everybody else out."

A Grieving Husband's Lament

WILLIAM PRICE CROSSED the Dollar General parking lot with a mischievous smile.

"Why don't you tell me a story," he said.

He'd seen the "Tell Me a Story" sign on the back of my bike, and he thought it would be funny to turn the tables on me.

Price was in Houston to lay flowers at his wife's graveside on her birthday. She recently died of cancer. She was dying of cancer that whole first year of the pandemic.

When people get Covid, they're not sure if they'll die. But they both knew that final year she was living with a death sentence.

Price contracted Covid but "not that bad." Still, he didn't want to face it again, so he was vaccinated.

"When I would walked up an incline," he said, "I would absolutely wear out."

His daughter's family and grandchildren caught Covid while traveling to Florida. Their experience was worse than his, but they recovered too.

At age 80, he was a retired local meat cutter still proud of his physical prowess.

"I could take 50 pounds (with one arm) and lift it up 75 times," he said of his youth.

He was "hesitant to say" if most people he knew were masking or were vaccinated. He admitted he sometimes forgot he was in a pandemic.

"I just was wanting to visit my nephew, and I just forgot (about distancing)," he said. "And my daughter called me a while ago and told me, don't do it. Don't go out there. It just slips your mind."

He found the pandemic baffling. He was more consumed by his wife's illness and death.

The the end of the interview, I was packing up my gear when he kept talking about her death. There are worse things than dying of Covid but the grieving is the same and seems like it's forever.

Fresh grief kept him talking. Her touch. Her voice. Her smile.

"You know, I miss her touch the most," he said. "I miss coming in the house and her saying, 'What have you been up to?' with her big smile."

"Most Difficult Year I've Experienced"

WHEN PHILLIP MILLIGAN'S close friend died a couple of weeks ago, there was no funeral or memorial.

A resident of Eureka, Milligan was in Mountain Grove when I met him in a grocery store parking.

The deceased friend was married to the Milligan family's former babysitter. The couple was trying to do everything right. They were masking and going to vaccinate when possible. But they both got Covid, and her husband passed away, leaving two grown children and four grandchildren.

Unlike so many other patients forced to die alone during the pandemic, the husband was allowed visits from his wife because she was a recent pandemic survivor.

"It's probably been the most difficult year that I've experienced," he said. "You feel like you have this cloud hanging over your head for an entire year. It's very difficult."

The week I met Milligan was the anniversary of the CDC declaring Covid-19 a global pandemic.

Milligan was retired but taught music on the college level via Zoom all year. He supervised student teachers online. His wife had multiple sclerosis, so "we were very, very careful because it would not go well for her if she got it."

Both his daughters were in education. One daughter was a teacher, and the other was an administrator. The teacher was going back to the classroom that day.

Family gatherings for Christmas, Thanksgiving, and his grandson's 2nd birthday "were low key" due to distancing restrictions.

It was about a year since he saw many of the people in his praise team, the singers and musicians at his church.

"That praise team is a big part of my social life," he said. "We really haven't all been together for about a year."

His church "erred on the side of caution" when it came to attendance and singing. But caution became controversial.

"When we started back in person, we started back everyone wearing a mask, which we're still doing," he said. "Very limited attendance. We're a church of about 175 or 200. And we're probably only having 50 people. In fact, we usually have less than that."

Opinions over the science of Covid prompted a religious schism.

"We've actually had some families who disagreed with that approach and thought we should have opened sooner and have left our church," he said. "It will be interesting, once we open back up, to see who is still standing."

The pandemic didn't change how Milligan used his free time because his hobbies were music and bicycle riding. Both could be pursued on his own. He was also spending "more time together" with his wife.

The pandemic got him thinking more about mortality.

"I'm right at 60 years old, and you do start to think of your own mortality," he said. "And then you have something that happens that kills more than a half-million people in your country. And then you have something that starts to hit home like it did a couple of weeks ago. It does make you stop and ponder a little bit."

Later, on Route 60, I saw him honking at me from the frontage road. I stopped on the highway as cars and trucks passed by.

Milligan ran up an embankment to me on the highway shoulder.

As cars and trucks whizzed by, he handed me plastic zip ties. He'd driven back to his toolbox to get the zip ties to secure the bicycle rack on my rear wheel.

He didn't have to be asked for help. He felt we all should help each other through whatever this is.

Carefree Dancing and a Covid Party

"I NEVER WAS AFRAID OF IT," said Paula Clark, with a smile.

She was on a mid-day walk with a friend along Galloway Creek Greenway in Springfield.

"I guess that's because I don't watch the regular news channels at all. So I just had no fear of it. I had no fear before I got it."

Covid is an overblown pandemic, she believed. If she had her way, she'd unmask everybody and let nature take its natural course.

"I was going out and going to dances, without masks," she said. "I know there were people who thought that wasn't a good behavior. It wasn't fair to other people. I felt like, other people are out there dancing. They feel the same way I do … that this is not that scary of a thing. If we are willing to expose ourselves to it, that shouldn't bother anybody else."

Others were bothered.

Be it from her boyfriend or her unmasked dances, she contracted Covid. Then she went to a family dinner party where she infected her daughter, son-in-law, and her six-year-old granddaughter. They spread it to her niece two days later.

"We didn't hug or kiss," she said, "but apparently just being in the room, I gave it to them."

Her symptoms were a stomach ache and a "low-grade" fever. It was milder than the flu, but it seemed to go on "forever." She stayed in bed when she was most sick.

After realizing that Covid had spread throughout the family, they decided to double down and hold another family party.

"What we did was have a Covid party," she said. "My son-in-law came and got me. We'd just sit around and watch TV ... We all stayed at their house for four or five days (along with another family friend)."

"I don't feel it is dangerous," she said. "I understand that other people are very fearful."

When I told her the latest pandemic death total, she doubted the official government statistics.

"But why aren't there any reports of the flu?" she said. "What happened to the people who died from the flu every year? I guess I don't trust the tests either, that they are completely reliable."

She read that people "must have some sort of pre-condition" in order for Covid to be severe or deadly.

"A normal, healthy person," she said, "I don't think should be worried."

Her boyfriend's roommate died of Covid. She didn't say who likely gave it to the roommate.

"You have to keep in mind, he was 82 years old," she said. "He had diabetes. He wasn't taking care of himself. And he already did not want to live before he ever got Covid."

She felt most other people were uninformed about the pandemic. However, she masked up when in stores out of respect for other people's feelings.

"I try to be respectful to people who are fearful," she said. "But I also feel so sorry for people who are so afraid of something that for a normal, healthy person, it's not anything more to be afraid of than you would be of the regular flu that kills people."

She didn't want to vaccinate but said she will get the shot if she needs one to fly on a commercial flight.

"But I've had it already," she said, exasperated. "And I know if I tell anybody, they'll say, 'But you can get it again.'"

She didn't know how the pandemic would go in the future, but she knew what people should do in the meantime.

"If I were in charge," she said, "I would unmask everybody. I know that sounds heartless. I'd just let people build up their immunities and let it run its course, like we do with regular flus."

Drama & Risks of Pandemic Reporting

THE SHEER SIZE and scope of a once-in-a-century pandemic was a reporting challenge he didn't see coming, said Steven Pokin, a Springfield columnist for the *News Leader*.

"When Covid hit a year ago, I was like many people, I thought it'd be a stronger version of the flu," he said. "I had no idea what was in store."

However, his job meant he was putting himself out there covering the pandemic. He masked, vaccinated, and distanced, but he was still out meeting people for stories.

One day, he was covering a protest rally on businesses shutting down. A protester was telling him the pandemic was a hoax.

At some point in the interview, he realized reporting the story might be endangering himself and his family.

"She was talking so loudly, at one point I feel the spit coming out of her mouth hitting my hand and my forearm," he said. "And that made me think, what risk is there to that? Should I be doing this?"

Of the pandemic stories he'd already covered, one tragedy stood out.

"I think the story I'll most remember is, I did a feature story on a woman named Angela Hughes who lived in Republic, still lives in Republic," he said. "And four generations of her family contracted Covid at the same time, including her. And she was very, very sick. Her grandfather survived. Her mother died. And her two children had contracted the disease and had mild symptoms. So it was the full range of the impact on the family."

Pokin was distancing by choice and by circumstance. A combination of the pandemic and a shrinking of the newspaper business meant that the *News Leader*'s newsroom was "cavernous." He canceled a retirement party for a co-worker at his home. He spent Thanksgiving with his immediate family.

He and his family hadn't contracted Covid, but his Chicago aunt died from it. A jogging friend got Covid and recovered.

"You never realize how your life is going to be impacted," he said. "And what are you going to do. Who are you going to see."

He did not believe the pandemic was unduly affecting his stress levels or happiness. He masked up and went to restaurants. He continued his running routine, sometimes with friends.

As for the future, he was anticipating a renewed appreciation for seeing people and getting together. He looked forward to handshakes again, even if it meant annual booster shots.

He admired a friend's post after she received her shot. He recited it from memory.

"In memory of all those who lost their lives and all those in grief, and I think of them as I feel fortunate to get my shot today."

He paused and smiled.

"I think that's the way to do it."

"I could see her ... but I could not touch her"

"I GET EMOTIONAL," said Samuel "Stinger" Stanley, the charismatic, social media posting, manager of Bud's Bait in Carthage.

Stanley was a lively, talkative man with a social media following, but his voice cracked, and his eyes welled up when he talked about his near-death experience with Covid.

Part of the anguish came from the hospital isolation that kept him from loved ones - including his fiancée.

"The isolation was the worst part of the whole thing," he said. "My fiancée would come to the window ... I was like a monkey in a cage or a fish in a fishbowl ... I could see her out there, but I could not touch her."

He choked up when he thought about, his eyes welled up with tears.

"I could hear her through the phone on speaker but I couldn't touch her," he said, getting more emotional as he talked. "And being able to touch you is more important to me than being able to hear ya. And it's hard on ya. The isolation is the hardest part. In my opinion."

He was certain that this was the end.

"I absolutely thought I was going to die," he said.,

He believed he contracted the disease from an uncle who later died of the disease.

Stinger still had post-Covid symptoms, including memory loss, racing heartbeats, and lung problems. Then he lifted his shirt and showed the sensors on his chest.

"I'll have this the rest of my life," he said of his heart and lung problems.

Stinger's sense of humor was one of his most noticeable traits, but he regrets joking about Covid before he contracted the virus.

"It's no joke," he said. "Don't take it lightly."

His recovery was nothing short of a miracle, he believes.

"There's a miracle involved somewhere along the way," Stinger said.

People should adhere to distancing and masking mandates, he said. If not just for ourselves, but for those around us.

My bicycle broke in Carthage and I was walking the 15 miles toward Joplin when Stinger waved me in. He convinced a customer to drive me to the next bicycle shop in Webb City.

He was so open and dramatic during his interview, we've stayed in touch on social media, he continues to suffer health consequences and another close relative died of Covid.

He is a veteran of the 82nd Airborne Division of U.S. Army but he ended our interview with one of the most compassionate quotes of the entire trip. He urged people to vaccinate and distance because we are not alone in this world.

"We are here to love everybody and protect each other," he said. "We are our brother's keeper."

"I'm Trusting the Lord"

LINDA RUSSOW SAW me beside the road looking at my GPS outside Joplin. She stopped her vehicle and got out to bring me homemade cookies and a bottle of water.

She believed that her faith called on her to help strangers like me.

She knew people who died of Covid, but she hadn't had it yet. And she was unsure if she was going to get vaccinated.

"I'm trusting in the Lord," she said. "My daughter wants me to get the shot."

Russow was unsure of what to do because she was unsure of God's plan for her.

"God has sent me so many miracles in my life," she said. "God has taken care of me in so many ways."

Then she handed me several religious pamphlets for the ride.

"I'm relying on the Lord Jesus Christ who died for us," she said.

She was being taken care of, but she wasn't sure about me. So along with the homemade cookies and the water, she added a blessing for the road.

"God bless and keep you on your travels."

"I went to other lands, so I would never see that prophesy fulfilled, the abomination of my evil fate."
— **Sophocles, Greek tragedian author of Oedipus Rex, set during the Plague of Thebes**

"Thanks to the Interstate Highway System, it is now possible to travel across the country from coast to coast without seeing anything."
— ***Charles Kuralt, TV journalist and author of On the Road***

AS FATE WOULD HAVE IT

KANSAS

*R*oute 66 is just a 13-mile stretch through Kansas and was almost the end of the road for me.

America's Main Street is also the main tourist attraction of Galena.

A giant Route 66 ceramic tile mural adorns the side of a building next to the town square. "Greetings from Galena" is bannered across the top. It features a blue 1957 Chevrolet driving up the Galena main street toward the vastness of the Kansas rural landscape.

Once a mining boom town with 30,000 residents in the early 1900s, Galena had about 3,000 residents in the last census and was shrinking.

The town made it into the 2006 computer-generated Disney Pixar comedy *Cars*, which bemoaned the way interstates bypassed "real America." Many small towns along Route 66 memorialize their part in the flick.

As I rode down Galena's wide, empty main street, the back wheel on my bicycle wobbled and moaned. I had the tire and rim adjusted in Joplin. It was 120 miles to Tulsa and the next bicycle shop. Should I go back and get it fixed again?

I stopped at the only Mexican restaurant in Galena and ordered the burrito special for lunch to think over the latest turn of events.

When the waiter brought the bill, I fumbled and searched for my wallet. The wallet was gone. Had it fallen out of my fanny pack on the ride? I couldn't continue the ride without money or identification.

I called the motel I stayed at in Joplin. I called Debby Johnson, the co-owner of Specialized Bicycles. Both the hotel manager and Johnson searched their establishments and called back, feeling terrible for me.

I was on a lame bicycle, with no money and 1,900 miles to go.

Desperate, I decided to empty my bicycle packs on the sidewalk outside the Mexican restaurant. I was 100 percent certain the wallet was not there.

My wallet fell out of my jeans, and I nearly fell on the sidewalk in astonishment.

I paid for the burrito and interviewed the hostess. She was my only interviewee in Kansas. She believed God and fate guided her life, in good fortune and bad.

Religious fatalism is said to be common in the United States and across religious and ethnic lines. Nobody has yet studied whether religious fatalism prompts more people to take precautions or throw precautions to the wind.

The menagerie of motivations matter in pandemics.

If the waitress was correct, my wallet crisis took on a new meaning.

Fate determined that my wallet would be lost. Fate, not free will, made me search my bicycle packs even though I was certain it was not there. I wasn't making the choices, they were made for me before I was born.

The ride continued, of course. That was always going to happen anyway. Because that's the way fate works.

As they say in Kansas, c'est la vie.

"In the Book of Life"

ANDREA JOHNSON WAS at the front desk of Mi Torito Mexican Restaurant in Galena when I met her.

She was working two restaurant jobs during the pandemic. She worked maskless in Kansas and with a mask just five miles away in Missouri. It made a huge difference to her.

"I didn't have to wear a mask (today), hallelujah!" she said. "But in Joplin, I do. It's a violation of my rights for this Covid. So I get to breathe today."

I asked if she was against mask wearing.

"We do what we have to do," she said. "We do what we do. But if we don't have to, I love to take it off. Some people think they're protecting themselves by wearing it. And that's their personal choice. Some, they do it to help themselves, I guess."

Nobody in her personal circle contracted the disease.

"I work with the public, so I know people who have had it," she said. "It's a sad thing. People come and go. But this is a horrible thing. It really is."

Layoffs in the restaurant industry were common during the pandemic's first year, but she survived with just a short shutdown.

"We had to shut down around Thanksgiving time for two weeks," she said, "because some of the kitchen staff came in contact with Covid."

The pandemic changed the way restaurants did business.

"A lot of restaurants in the Joplin area have only drive-through and take-out orders," she said. "So, you can't sit down and dine in, which was a little bit of an effect in some restaurants. They have to social distance, so you can only have so much seating."

Family get-togethers were cut back.

"I think some families have had setbacks. Not getting as big a family gathering, you know. Because you can only have ten people or less. So I think some people are afraid to get too many people around."

She knew of a holiday gathering that turned deadly.

"I heard about an Italian family not too long ago that got together and like half the family passed away. You know, that's kinda sad to hear."

Her family holidays were the same as other years.

"We got together at Christmas time, but it wasn't a big deal. We only had a few family members. We are all fine."

She didn't suffer undue anxiety or unhappiness during the year.

"If you let fear control your life, you'll never get nowhere. I feel like I'm going to get up and go to work and do my daily things. And life goes on."

Religious fatalism was her way of dealing with the pandemic.

"Death is going to come. My time is already written down in the book of life. And there's not nothing I can do about it. God is on my side."

"There ain't no sin and there ain't no virtue. There's just stuff people do."
— **John Steinbeck, author of The Grapes of Wrath, suffered a near-fatal attack of the 1918 Spanish Flu.**

"Everybody's ignorant, only on different subjects."
— **Will Rogers, Oklahoma-native, commentator/humorist, whose two-year-old son Freddy died of the bacterial contagion diphtheria in 1918.**

THE MIND IS A FORCE OF NATURE

OKLAHOMA

Oklahoma-born folk singer Woody Guthrie wrote songs about the Dust Bowl. John Steinbeck wrote about it too. The Dust Bowl of the 1930s still stands as the greatest single man-made natural disaster in American history.

Yet the Covid pandemic has killed more people in Oklahoma than the Dust Bowl, more than double. Covid is an historic disaster but the Dust Bowl made for more dramatic photos.

I loved Oklahoma even as it suffered.

On two separate occasions, herds of grazing cows saw me riding by and began running beside me on the other side of a fence.

I rode past farms with chickens, pigs, cows, and cropland. A boy about seven years old ran with a bucket between the farmhouse and the barn. I knew there were factory farms somewhere but the view from Route 66 was like a time warp.

To nobody at all, I said, "Wow."

Every small town was a different sociological study. Every isolated ranch house looked like novels could be written about the families inside.

The oil fields, farms, pastures, big cities, and scores of small towns stretched out to far flat horizons. I rode into the sunset and camped in groves of trees at the edge of small towns at night.

I wondered if I could chuck it all and be happy in one of these small towns, far from the striving life. At times, I thought I could just live content inside a small-town dream in a windy, lovely land.

It's easy to fantasize, but the reality was that I also rode across Oklahoma on the 100th anniversary of the 1921 Tulsa Race Massacre. Thirty-plus people were killed that night, and another 800 more were hospitalized. The Cherokee Trail of Tears ended in Oklahoma. The trail from the Southeastern United States killed thousands, not surprisingly, mostly from disease.

About 1,370 miles of Route 66, or about half of the entire route, runs through Indian country. In 2022, the Supreme Court ruled that 43 percent of Oklahoma, including Tulsa, is on Indian land. The state hosts 39 separate Indian nations.

The road has historical markers and murals that celebrate scout/merchant Jesse Chisholm, athlete Jim Thorp, and the lesser known Andrew Harley Payne. He was the Cherokee American winner of the 1928 foot-race along the entire length of Route 66.

Humorist and social commentator Will Rogers was part Cherokee. He became known as "Oklahoma's Favorite Son." After he died in 1935, they officially designated Route 66 the Will Rogers Highway.

It was said of Rogers that he came from an ordinary background and that's why he could relate to ordinary people. Except nobody is ordinary.

His father, Clem, was half Cherokee and fought in the Civil War - as a Confederate officer and holder of two slaves. When Will Rogers was growing up, his father was a member of the Ku Klux Klan.

Oklahoma is a conservative "Bible Belt" state with a history of racial strife and Jim Crow laws.

The 2020 census showed the state is 72 percent White, 9 percent Native American, 9 percent Hispanic, and 7 percent Black. About 47 percent of Oklahomans say they're evangelical Christian, according to Pew Research. It's ranked 43rd in household income in the US.

I rode the length of Oklahoma, through Quapaw, Commerce,

Miami, Welch, Vinita, Chelsea, Catoosa, Claremore, Tulsa, Sapulpa, Bristow, Stroud, Chandler, Edmond, Oklahoma City, El Reno, Hydro, Clinton, Yukon, Sayre, Canute, Elk City, and Erick and to the border of the Texas panhandle.

Will Rogers once said, "I never met a man I didn't like."

Will Rogers expected to find good people, and found them. I held the same expectations and found the good is the norm.

I rode frontage roads and back roads the length of Oklahoma along Tornado Alley. I thought about the past and all the contradictions of race, religion, and income inequality. The past didn't seem so past.

It's still the land of strong opinions and wind. Dust storms and pandemics are forces of nature and so is the human brain. Our opinions are fueled by luck, nurture and nature.

And nature in Oklahoma is tornado prone.

Song of the Cricket

SHORTLY AFTER CROSSING from Kansas into Oklahoma, I rode without fear of traffic toward the center of Quapaw, pop. 858.

It's a financially struggling small town on the plains. About 40 percent of its kids live in poverty. About a fifth of the population is Native American.

Born and raised in Chicago, Alfred "Cricket" Rice was wearing a Chicago Cubs jacket while at the outdoor service window of Dallas' Dairyette.

After Cricket put down his food, he served up pandemic stories so stunning that I had to pause for a few moments before continuing.

I asked if any of his family or friends got sick or died of Covid.

"Actually, within my family, we've had roughly about 19 people pass away from it - within the past eight months," Cricket said. "Great aunts. Great uncles. And a couple of cousins. And, actually, I've had close friends who passed away from it, at my age."

How does a person handle that kind of death toll in a single year?

"Well, it's not pleasant," he said. "Actually, it's a loss of history. A lot of the people who are now gone from Covid, we actually learned our history from, our culture."

I asked if the astonishing number of deaths caused him excessive anxiety, stress or pain. What does going through a year like that do to his happiness?

"That's a good question," he said. "I guess the best way to answer that is just to prepare for the future. Take care of what you have. Appreciate all that you have. Just make it the best way you can ... And with all the elders passing now, a lot of us now have to step up and take their place."

He'd already made tribal references, so I asked if Quapaw was on tribal land.

"A matter of fact, you are," he said. "The Quapaw tribe of Indians originated from, oh geez, North Dakota, South Dakota. And migrated their way down to present day Quapaw, Oklahoma."

Native Americans were acutely aware of their vulnerability during pandemic times. An estimated 90 percent of the Indians in North America were wiped out by smallpox, measles, and flu cases after they came in contact with the White Europeans.

The toll on Native Americans was far harsher than the general US population, according to a Princeton University study released in 2021. Higher rates of poverty, overcrowding, and the lack of nearby, high-quality medical facilities were cited in the report.

"The majority of us, when it first got started, we kind of knew what to expect, and we just kind of started sticking to one another," he said. "Basically, avoiding going out and doing things. Getting all the supplies we're going to need and basically staying at home.

"However, you can't stay at home forever. Individuals went to stores and things like that and were catching it from other individuals. We did take precautions. Unfortunately, it didn't work out."

Tribal leaders were trying to get in front of the outbreak but the community was still being devastated. I asked about the vaccination rate.

"Actually, there is (a high vaccination rate)," he said. "The majority of the tribes, for example, the tribe I represent is the Sac & Fox nation out of Stroud, Oklahoma. All of our tribal individuals have been getting together with their elders and individuals who are at high risk. And first responders, that sort of thing, all the way down to our children, are all now vaccinated. The majority of the tribes of northeastern Oklahoma are now vaccinated. As a matter of fact, the tribes got together and, seeing how bad of a pandemic this was, just decided to do something about it before it even got worse."

He lauded the vaccinations but seemed to suggest a "positive outlook" helps ward off Covid too.

"I'd say the vaccination rate is probably up about 98 percent," he said. "Myself, I don't really utilize a mask because I don't really go anywhere. Other than just around town and back home. But as far as the future goes, you should just prepare and have a positive outlook."

He was a car salesman, so I asked how his business was going.

"Oddly enough, it's actually picked up," he said. "Because a majority of your customers really don't like to come and deal with the hassle of sitting around all day to purchase a vehicle. So what I've done is utilize the internet, social media, and customer contact directory. I'll meet them at the dealership and in 30 minutes to an hour, sign the papers, and we're good to go."

On a scale of 1 to 10, with 10 being the best, I asked him how the pandemic was going for him.

"On a personal basis, I'd say probably about a two," he said. "However … just the way people live and how they look at things, I'd have to rate it as high as 10. Because it's made people come together and yet had them wake up."

Given all that's happened, I asked what he thought was next.

"That's a good question," he said. "I guess the best way I can answer that clearly is to simply say, be kind to one another. Do what it is you're supposed to do. Don't waste your life. Just be aware."

Small Town Mayor Listens to the People

WINSTON MCKEON WASN'T GOING to mention he was mayor of Welch until a woman in a nearby parked car mentioned that I'd chosen the perfect person to talk to about Covid in Welch, pop. 622.

Welch is a bedroom community for nearby medical facilities. Unlike many rural towns, Welch is well situated for severe Covid cases. However, agriculture is the main business, with ranching and the raising of grains, corn, wheat, and soybeans.

"I think our isolated, rural location has saved us from waves (of Covid)," McKeon said, adding that vaccination outreach in the area was good. "My wife and I are vaccinated."

Isolation may be what this pandemic called for but it is the single worst part of life in a pandemic.

When it came time to bury the dead, the people of Welch struggled with the national guidelines calling for isolation during funeral services.

"We have people that think that with some of the chemicals they deal with as they work their cattle and their other agricultural endeavors, gives them some sort of immunity boost against the virus," he said. "So there have been some indoor services, but for the most part, people have done outside graveside (funerals)."

When the pandemic started almost exactly a year ago, the mayor pushed for guidance from the CDC and Republican Governor Kevin Stitt's office. He encouraged social distancing and avoiding large groups.

Compliance with the distancing guidelines was "political," he said, mirroring national political trends.

"People are fairly independent in our area," he said. "To begin with, it kinda fell along political lines. If you think this way, you wear a mask. If you think that way, don't wear a mask. So we have that cross-section happening here as well."

McKeon knew people who were vigilant about masks who got sick and people who never wore a mask who escaped infection.

He was isolating his wife in their home, his "cave," he called it.

They discouraged their children from Texas and Tennessee from visiting. He taught music at the local high school and played professionally before becoming mayor. When the pandemic hit, he was already retiring as a music teacher. He found staying home easy and limiting trips to the grocery store.

"Now that we have a vaccination, we are considering going to see (his children)," he said.

On a happiness scale of 1 to 10, he said his pandemic year was around a 5. He was more worried about the long-term and wider implications of the disease.

"It's been a year, for me personally," he said. "Our country and our school children are going to be impacted for a long time."

He hoped vaccinations will usher the way out of the crisis.

If that's what it takes, the mayor of Welch said he was fine with isolating for a while longer.

"I think vaccinations are going to be essential to finding a way back to normalcy," he said. "I'm still not going to hang out with people I don't hang out with. And like I said, I'm pretty comfortable with that already ... Are we going to mask for the rest of our lives? I don't know. They've been doing it in the orient for a while. We'll see what happens."

"Everyone is just so much more friendly."

DANIELLE HEWITT GOT COVID, lost her job, and even though it seems counterintuitive, she thought the pandemic might just be making people friendlier.

Life was pretty good in 2020. She had an exciting job in Tulsa's thriving film/music industry and a great apartment.

Then she fell ill. At first, her test gave a false negative, but then all the telltale symptoms kicked in.

"I lost my (sense of) smell," she said. "I lost my taste. I felt like I'd been hit by a truck, and I kept working. I'd sleep for 30 minutes. Wake up and work for like an hour. Sleep for 30 minutes. Just to get through it."

Both her parents and her brother contracted Covid. Her best friend probably did too. That's her social "bubble."

"Then 2021 hit, and everything kinda went downhill for me," she said. "I worked in film and music, and unfortunately, those areas are very affected by Covid. Unfortunately, my job was no longer necessary."

Yet something strange and unexpected was afoot. When she walked her dogs, she noticed people being friendlier.

"Everyone is just so much more friendly," she said. "People will go out of their way to wave at you, on their porches. Ask you how you're doing. Everyone, of course, stays away from each other but ... the human contact ... everyone is just so excited we're seeing the light at the end of the tunnel."

She held high hopes that the end might come by the summer of 2021. If only enough people vaccinate, mask and distance. Her entire family was vaccinated.

She didn't want to "get political," but she wanted to see people cooperating to help stem the effects of the pandemic.

"I think we just need to keep wearing the masks," she said. "And keep on the regulations. And I think by summer, we'll be ready to go."

Pandemic Drives People to the Outdoor Life

TULSA'S cultural and economic vitality was under pressure during the worst of the pandemic, and lifestyles adapted to the new realities.

The outdoor lifestyle business seemed made for the socially distancing, and J. P. Hewitt's The Gadget Company store thrived. A born entrepreneur, Hewitt's real estate, hunting, and ranching businesses did well too.

"Business has been very good for us, we've been very lucky," he said. "People aren't traveling as much. I think they have money to spend locally, that they'd normally spend on trips. And they want to get out and do outdoor activities because it's a socially distanced event or sport or whatever that may be."

The Gadget Company store closed for a couple of months, and he had to cut hours for employees, but the store bounced back.

"Tulsa has supported us through all that," he said.

He believed he was the first in his family to get Covid and passed it along to his sister, both parents, and his girlfriend.

Thanksgiving and Christmas holidays were curtailed. Get-togethers were cut back. He didn't go to as many events as he did pre-pandemic.

"Which made it really difficult because nobody understood anything," he said. "Nobody knew what was going on."

Hewitt worried about his business and the health of everyone he loved.

"In the beginning, it was really stressful," he said. "I couldn't see my girlfriend nearly as much because she is an ER nurse, so she was on the front lines with everybody."

The last year or so was a rollercoaster as far as his personal happiness during the pandemic.

As for the future, he hoped for the best.

"I don't know, but I hope this is going in the direction where this is going to all be over pretty soon, and we can get back to what used to be a normal life. And be able to travel again. And see friends again, regularly. Eat out. Support local restaurants."

The Tulsa music scene, which the city is known for, is something he really missed during the pandemic.

Route 66 and music played a key role in the development of modern Tulsa. The "Father of Route 66" Cyrus Avery came from Tulsa. The town's ballrooms were famous stopping points. The city's reputation as one of the greatest talent pools for musicians and music dates back to its early reputation as a center for Western Swing.

"One thing I noticed the other day is we haven't been to a concert or some kind of music event in a really long time," he said. "And that has really been weird. Because that has always been a big part of Tulsa, I feel like, music and outdoor activities like that."

"If I'm going to die, I'm (dying) in Oklahoma!"

AS A HEAVY EQUIPMENT SALESMAN, John Morton traveled about 300 nights a year.

One night in Alabama, he and a friend were at a restaurant together having dinner. While waiting for the check, he felt Covid sweep over him.

"I start coughing. I get the chills. I say (to my friend) take me back to the hotel, I'm not feeling too good."

On his third day of suffering, he manages to drive to a hospital 60 miles away. Someone at the hospital told him he had the symptoms, but they couldn't confirm it, and he didn't need hospitalization yet.

"So I went back to the hotel, lay in the hotel for two nights and wake up and say, 'If I'm going to die, I'm going to die in Oklahoma!'" he said. "So I take off for Oklahoma."

It took three days of driving with severe symptoms before he arrived home in Chandler. He lay half dead in bed for another four days. On his doctor's advice, he was off work for three weeks.

He resisted wearing a mask until shortly before he caught Covid. He didn't think it helped at all.

"Before, I wasn't masking, and I'm not going to mask now," he said. "I feel like the masks we're using, they aren't going to protect anything. They say you gotta have those N-95 masks, and the masks people are wearing aren't doing anything. And most of the people you see, the masks they're wearing are underneath their noses. That's not going to do anything either. So why wear a mask?"

He believed he'd found a loophole in pandemic restrictions because he packs a handgun. Wearing a mask while armed is illegal.

"It's a federal law. For me carrying a gun, I would be a convicted felon to do it, so I'm not going to be a convicted felon,"

He claimed he wasn't getting a vaccine because the FDA hadn't yet given its final approval for them, only emergency approval.

"Right now, I do not trust the government," he said. "If y'all come back as zombies, I'm going to shoot you in the head (smiling at his own sense of humor). That's the redneck in me coming out ... I don't trust what the government's doing right now."

He knew the dangers. He had friends who died and a co-worker who was flown to Colorado for treatment.

No masking, distancing, or vaccinations for him despite his near-death experience.

His business took a 38 percent dive when the pandemic hit.

He didn't know what will happen in the future with Covid, saying the "government" was wrong about the pandemic in the past. He claimed the government promised the pandemic was going away in the summer of 2020.

"They have no idea what's going on now."

So in the immediate future, he was armed but not against Covid.

Owners Suffer Covid while Motel Thrives

THE PANDEMIC LOOMED large over Sam Patel's family-run Red Carpet Inn in Edmond.

Seven of the eight people in his family at the Red Carpet contracted the disease. Everyone but his three-year-old daughter. But nobody in the family required hospital care. They all intended on getting vaccinations as soon as they were able.

"It did bring us (our family) a lot closer this year," he said.

The business part of the family business thrived.

"Our business has been better during Covid," he said. "Because we're kind of a local motel, and we're not worried about tourism and things like that. So a lot of the local people stay here on a weekly, monthly basis. We did get a lot of new customers from that."

As for lessons learned from the year, he said, "just clean, sanitize."

"There's just nothing you can really do with an outbreak like that," he said. "I guess that humanity worked together and did kinda defeat Covid somewhat. I know we're still working on it."

He thought the vaccines might eradicate the pandemic within the next ten years or so.

"I think the vaccines will be an ongoing thing for the next few years if not longer," he said. "Things like this, like the flu, don't just go away in a year's time, especially when it conquered the whole world. So I think with vaccines, in ten years, Covid won't be any kind of issue whatsoever."

He was no fan of how the Trump Administration handled the outbreak.

"The new administration (response to Covid) has been appropriate. The old administration was not at all. I think they made matters worse, and then they did better. But I guess you live and you learn. And hopefully, the government will learn from their mistakes as well."

After the camera turned off, I followed up on an earlier question about their business thriving during the pandemic. Patel gave credit to the government stimulus checks because the homeless of Edmond used them for temporary housing.

"When the stimulus checks come in ... they need a place to stay. They'd come here and get a place to stay for a week or however much they could to kinda help set themself up to get a job or have an address to get a job. Stimulus checks did help our business by giving them a place to stay and a way to start over."

Marine Lived "extremely difficult" Year

TYLER REICH WAS a Marine who served internationally but returned to a pandemic battlefield at home.

Reich's home was Yukon, the home of musician Garth Brooks and

Yukon's Best Flour mill.

Reich's father was getting over hepatitis C when he caught Covid and later developed pneumonia. When the hospital sent his father home, despite suffering from multiple ailments, Reich went to live with his father as a caregiver. Reich calls the hospital's decision to send his father home "ridiculous."

"They sent him home (alone)," he said. "He had no one to take care of him, so I had to go down there and help him out. It was extremely hard because you're trying not to catch it just like everyone else out here, but at the same time, you have to take care of your family. And you're in the same house with someone with such a deadly disease. So it's pretty terrible."

The experience was "extremely difficult."

"It left him with breathing problems," he said. "Luckily, he got over it. But it just demolished his immune system."

Tyler Reich worked at a trailer company, building custom trailers with 300 other workers. He wore masks and distanced. But people worked close to each other. A 24-year-old co-worker contracted the disease and died six days later.

He believed cooperating with pandemic restrictions was his responsibility to his family.

"I have a 4-year-old," he said. "You can't risk those kinda things."

Distancing didn't bother him because of his experiences with foreign deployments in the Marines. But his wife was very "family oriented" and social so she found it "very difficult." .

Asked if anything good happened in the first year of the pandemic, he pointed to the transient nature of life and the importance of "loving" each other.

"I think making people more aware of loving each other and being close to each other because you never know how much longer somebody can truly be around," he said. "I think that's a good thing that came from this."

He thought pandemic restrictions might be ongoing. More people are going to get vaccinated, and "this is pretty close to being the new norm."

With the United States leading the world with pandemic deaths, he said the government handled the pandemic "pretty poorly."

"They shoved money into people's pockets and expect that to make your life easier," he said. "Money can't solve everything, as a lot of people know."

He worried about "super-adverse effects" of the vaccine. He heard that "people have died from the vaccine." He pointed to the case of "a guy in South Dakota" that died of a vaccine.

"I don't think they've done a good job of containing it, because it spread across the whole freakin' world," he said. "So I don't think they've done a very good job at it."

He pointed to China as an example of how lockdowns work. As a Marine, he worked in Asia, and their lockdowns have contained pandemics far better than in the USA.

"I think," he said, "other countries have had a better way of containing it than we have."

Long-Haul Covid "Changed my life"

LUPE NICHOLAS VIDAURRI was living with the uncertainty of whether he'd ever be the person he once was.

He was a happy person before getting ill. When I spoke to him, he wondered if he'll ever be happy again.

I met the Sayre resident at a Canute gas station. After contracting Covid at the nursing home where he was working, his long-haul symptoms changed his life.

"It was bad," he said. "Very scary. Very scary for me. I still have problems with it. I think it affected my mentality. I suffer from depression. I think it messed with my eyes. It's bad."

He received two weeks off to recover at his home. His two daughters and brother got Covid too. He not only feared for his life, but those of his daughters and brother.

"It changed my life," he said. "I was very positive ... It's changed my outlook in life."

As for how the government responded to the pandemic, he said, "I'm pro-Trump."

He was vaccinated, and work required a mask, but he didn't mask if he didn't have to.

"I don't really mask anymore since I've already had Covid and I already had the vaccine," he said. "I kinda put my guard down, which I shouldn't."

Vidaurri grew tired of talking about it and abruptly ended the interview.

When I left him, he was standing alone, leaning against the gasoline station wall, gazing out at the horizon lost in thought.

Rancher says Cattle De-Wormer Saved His Life

JERRY SPITZ ASSUMED I knew all about Ivermectin use in rural America. So he launched into his story of how he used his cattle dewormer as a lifesaving cure for Covid.

I had not heard of it. It became national news later in the summer of 2021, when late-night TV comedians began joking about rural people who, in desperation, turned to the drug to save their lives.

From where I stood in rural Oklahoma, a dying person resorting to such a risky folk remedy was no joke. People saw their ER rooms overflowing and tests took a week or more.

In the meantime, rural people were dying from lack of care or seeking alternative medicines.

An occupational therapist by training, Jerry Spitz was a partially disabled rancher when his brush with the disease nearly killed him. His son, daughter-in-law, and grandson already contracted Covid. He used his occupational therapy training when he ran out of traditional options.

He felt like he was dying, slipping away by the hour. He was horrified to see that his oxygen levels were plummeting.

"On Christmas Eve, about two o'clock in the morning, I had a lot of trouble breathing," he said. "So I called the ER. It felt like my heart was going to fall out of my chest. So I go over to the ER, and they were so busy. One of the nurses came outside and said ... they're not going to do nothing for ya."

He drove home from the hospital, his heart still pounding, believing he was going to die at any moment.

"A guy who butchers my cattle calls me in the middle of the night because he found out a day or two before that I had Covid," he said. "One of his best friends passed away. He said, 'You need to take Ivermectin tonight. Don't horse around. I can't believe you haven't took it.'"

Spitz was sicker than he'd ever been and felt he might die that night.

"So about three o'clock in the morning, I go out in the barn and find some injectable Ivermectin," he said. "I didn't know what it would taste like, so I figured, I'll just dose it out like I would a cow, by my weight. So I thought, why don't you take 2 cc's?"

He took a dose based on his weight and mixed it with apple juice. On Christmas Day, he felt "so good, I didn't mess with it." He didn't take another dose.

The day after Christmas, he again took a dramatic turn for the worse.

"All that crap comes back again, only worse," he said. "I had trouble breathing. My heart rate was way up."

This time he took Ivermectin and dexamethasone, a steroid he gives his cattle when they have breathing problems. The anticipation must have been intense.

Was he using the right amount? Would the cure kill him?

"In about four hours, I could start breathing a whole lot easier," he said. "So the next day, I did the same thing again ... And, hell, I felt great! ... I was feeding cattle and doing everything like it was nothing."

On that Monday, he got the week-old Covid test back. It showed he'd been positive. The results came back after the crisis that might have killed him. He went to see his doctor to tell him what he'd done.

"I figured I'd get a butt chewin' for what I done," he said. "I just told him what I did. And he just was very matter of fact, that that's what a lot of people's done. And they've had good results. And he was more inquisitive to how much I took. Why I took that much. He was just trying to get a feel for what people was takin'."

Spitz later said the Ivermectin also dewormed him. He found a six-inch green worm in his toilet one day.

He added that his veterinarian gave him a clean Ivermectin bottle, in case Covid returns to him or one of his family. Going out to the barn at 2 a.m. to take medicine, the veterinarian said, isn't sanitary.

Spitz didn't intend to get the vaccine. If he gets Covid again, he'll rely on Ivermectin again.

"They (at his doctor's office) asked me if I was going to take the shot, and I said, 'No,' because Ivermectin kicked it in the butt," he said. "I don't see any use in taking the vaccine."

His risk of getting the disease again was low, he predicted, because he was already socially distanced out on the ranch.

Cattle dewormer and steroids weren't the only folk remedies locals were taking. He knew people who took hydroxychloroquine, recommended by President Trump. The drug has repeatedly been tested and proven ineffective.

Then he stepped back to look at the big picture.

"The whole deal, you look at Pfizer, you look at Bill Gates, a lot of that just don't make sense," he said, referring to a false conspiracy theory that Gates implanted a tracking system in vaccines. "Right now, Fauci, he changes his mind like the way the wind blows here in Oklahoma. That's every 30 minutes."

Spitz trusted President Trump for leadership on the pandemic. Trump, he believed, was also trying to prevent panic by being "quiet" on some subjects.

If President Biden had managed the early stages of the pandemic, "There's no telling what might have happened." He worried about socialism taking over America.

He knew "fifty people off the top of my head who's had" Covid, including his sister, two brothers-in-law, two stepdaughters, and some of their kids.

"I know some people who've died from it," he said. "The ones that died from it, hell, they had one leg and hip in the grave ... they were in bad, sad shape."

Asked if his personal happiness had been altered by the virus, he mentioned his fear of Chinese chemical warfare.

"Yes, it scared the crap out of me," he said. "You always wonder if this was some sort of chemical warfare. Different people was gettin' it, and different people was dyin'. And the TV makes everything ten times worse than it is."

It was unclear which TV station he was referring to.

"The way I look at it," he said, "the good Lord put us on this earth for so long, and when my time is coming, he's going to take me out anyway."

(Half of what you read was deleted by YouTube. All interviews are on the University of Florida's SPOHP archive site.)

Pot Smoking Performance Artist Talks Covid

I WALKED into the Sandhill Curiosity Shop in Erick and was blown away.

"And now it looks as though they're here to stay, oh, I believe in YESTERDAY!"

Standing in the center of a densely cluttered room in his ripped and torn blue jean bib overalls with a long gray beard and a jack-o'-lantern smile, Harley Russell was singing as loudly as he could into a microphone to an audience on none.

He kept playing as if I was invisible in his performance theater of the redneck mind. His place was a hoarder's dream, with Route 66, Greyhound Bus, Coca-Cola, Mobil Oil and Texaco signs willy-nilly around the room. There was homemade artwork, a stage, and tables with half-full bottles of booze on them for passing strangers.

The sign outside read: "WELCOME TO ERICK, OKLAHOMA - THE REDNECK CAPITAL OF THE WORLD - HEE-HAW!"

A sign below it read: "SEE REDNECKS WORK AND PLAY IN THEIR OWN ENVIRONMENT."

When Harley stopped singing, he kept up his performance.

"I'm Harley Russell. I'm right here in Erick, Oklahoma, the Redneck Capital of the World," he said before the first question is asked. "Ninety-nine percent of my customers come from overseas. So they didn't come over (in) the last year. I'm going to tell you what happened. The Americans got cabin fever, and they couldn't sit still in a room by themselves ... So they got out on the road and came to see me."

Harley depended on tips for his singing and performance art. He showed me the shop and told me of his heartbreak when his wife Annabell died (giving new meaning to his singing The Beatles hit "Yesterday" to himself).

"In spite of Covid, I had a good year," he said. "So doctor Fauci ouchie doesn't get fucking nothing from me. And neither does anybody else because I just got my shot last week. And I had all kinds of people come in here, and I didn't even catch V.D. (venereal disease)."

He entertained the public in his small shop, so he wasn't social distancing or masking. He was 74 years old and would be considered at high risk, yet he hadn't gotten the disease and didn't know anyone who did. He was vaccinated and thought little of anti-vaxxers.

"Have you ever heard of something called common sense?" he said. "Well, common sense would tell you, if you look at the statistics, and I got the Johnson & Johnson ... if you didn't take the vaccine, you'd be an idiot."

Then he brings up politics.

"Two weeks after last year's election is when the vaccine started pouring out. Just to make sure you motherfuckers get your facts straight. Don't try to talk me down because I am a political fucking genius."

He thought Covid would go away "but not very silently" in "no more than five years."

Then he lit up a marijuana joint, took a puff, and pontificated about big government's response to the pandemic.

"Big government responds to the reactions they get from the American public," he said. "They do not respond to Covid. They go with what will be politically correct for them."

I asked about his sense of happiness during pandemic times.

"You gotta be kiddin' me," he said. "The state of the world is going to affect my happiness? I do not think so. That is the problem most people have. Including you dorks in education land ... Geographic location has nothing to do with happiness. What people think of you has nothing to do with happiness (unless you're feeding your ego like most of you are). But you (should) depend on no one to feed you with happiness."

He considered him an expert on happiness.

"Happiness is just something you just have," he said. "And that is developed through a long period of grief, sorrow, and all kinds of inward battles that you can develop your own vaccine against once you start participating in the now, the moment, the mindfulness perception, self-observation. Like I said, 99 percent of the people are in the past or the future. And those people sadly (mistake) activity and acquisition as a form of happiness."

The pandemic didn't dent his happiness. He had his traveling audiences and weed.

"So did (it affect) me, sorry, baby, but it didn't affect me."

He'd been discovered by a select group of filmmakers, travel writers, and European media, so he drew visitors from around the world. If European tourism drops, he predicted Americans will be traveling more in the USA.

In the meantime, he was defiant in an insane world. His wild man performance art was his rebellion.

Yet was it a performance?

Before I left, he sang to a private audience of one, a rousing version of "Route 66."

"The coronavirus panic is dumb."
— **Billionaire Elon Musk, founder of Austin, Tx.-based Tesla
Inc. Musk suffered two bouts of Covid-19, once after
vaccination.**

*"When I think of death, I only regret that I will not be able
to see this beautiful country anymore unless the Indians are
right and my spirit will walk here after I'm gone."*
— **Georgia O'Keeffe, artist, was teaching outside Amarillo
when she caught the Spanish Flu and saw her chance for love.
While ill, she moved to Manhattan so photographer Alfred
Sieglitz could nurse her back to health. They later married.**

PANHANDLE WITH CARE

TEXAS

*I*n the small Texas Panhandle town of Mclean, there's a sign above a classic Route 66 diner.

"Chuckwagon 'So good it'll make your spurs spin.'"

Inside there's a full Route 66 roadmap across an entire wall with the words "The Mother Road" next to the sexy cartoon character Betty Boop driving a red convertible. Chicken fried steak and milkshakes are specialties.

The waitress behind the counter, Mallory, screamed in mock horror and hung up the phone before serving me.

"That was Colleen, the owner," she said, explaining milkshakes take a long time to make right.

"She prank called me. She asked for 11 milkshakes, all flavors. I thought, 'Oh no! I'm going down!'"

She laughed as if we were old friends.

"Whatcha gonna have?"

Mclean, pop. 778, is rooted in the real panhandle cowboy, rancher, and Indian lore. It's one the High Plains, with miles of acacia, mesquite, and cacti. It's informally known as the Llano Estacado, or the Stakes Plains, because travelers by horse were forced to drive stakes into the ground to show the way across.

When I rode across the panhandle, conservative politics made masking and vaccines controversial. Yet Texas was once at the forefront of pandemic science. In 1898 and 1899, a smallpox outbreak in Laredo led to the state-appointed version of Dr. Fauci to order compulsory vaccinations. He made home quarantines and fumigation mandatory. Contaminated clothes were ordered to be burned. The Texas Rangers were called to Laredo to enforce the law.

The ensuing Laredo Smallpox Riot led to shoot-outs between Texas Rangers and rioters. Two men were killed and dozens injured. The quarantines and vaccinations eventually worked. The smallpox outbreak that threatened the entire state was contained.

Except for Amarillo, the north Texas Panhandle is a severe, underpopulated stretch of land. The farming practices of early settlers led to that part of Texas being among the hardest hit by the Dust Bowl.

Historic Route 66 straddles cattle and oil country on the Texas Panhandle. I rode the 160-mile width of the panhandle, visiting Shamrock, McLean, Conway, Amarillo, Vega, Adrian, and to the border of New Mexico. Texas has the most ghost towns in the country, with 511 once-flourishing towns.

An estimated 88 percent of all cattle under feed in Texas are in the panhandle. It's the largest cattle state with 13 million cattle which yearly produce waste the size of a city of 44.6 million people.

There are more cows than people in this part of the world, and about half of the people are non-Hispanic White. The voting record in those parts was overwhelmingly conservative.

Although the land use in Texas is cattle oriented, Texas is a $2 trillion diversified economy, bigger than Brazil. About 77 percent of Texans said they were Christians, and more than a third said they were evangelical Christians.

Underfoot, the Ogallala Aquifer is the largest aquifer in the country, spreading across eight states and almost the entire panhandle. It's fast being depleted by agricultural, livestock, and human activity, and in 2021 it dropped a foot.

After staying a night in a cheap Amarillo motel and filing my videos online, I rode out the next day to spend most of it at the #1 tourist attraction of Route 66, the Cadillac Ranch.

The ranch features ten vintage fan-tailed Cadillacs buried nose deep in a Texas dirt pasture. Tourists use spray paint cans to paint messages on the hard ground and to decorate the cars.

I bicycled slowly for a couple of days and cursed the wind as distances grew between small towns and water. Insane Texas ranch dogs chased me. Interstate 40 traffic and freight trains powered alongside the two-lane Historic Route 66. Hundreds of black-tailed prairie dogs beside the road ran panicky around their prairie dog towns.

I rode past thousands of cattle in feedlots. The average panhandle feedlot holds about 26,000 cattle.

Mounting environmental problems, a struggling oil/gas industry, diminishing groundwater, and an extended drought added environmental uncertainty to the stressors of the pandemic.

Yet most people weren't living in mortal fear, they were adjusting.

After all, there's a town in Texas where you can find the perfect chicken fried steak and old-fashioned milkshakes. The laughing waitress will treat you like a friend and bring you food so good it makes your spurs spin.

"I'm a personal contact person"

LOUISIANA MACHINE SHOP owner Timothy Kyle in Amarillo came to see the Cadillac Ranch for some light-hearted entertainment in a heavy-hearted time.

The Cadillac Ranch features ten Cadillacs buried hood-first in a cow pasture beside historic Route 66 and I-40.

The Cadillacs, from the 1940s to 1960s, are lined up in a row. It's a short dirt walk from the highway. Visitors are encouraged to spray-paint bright-colored graffiti on the cars and on the dirt pathway.

It's the #1 tourist attraction along Route 66, with graffiti opinions from around the country. Kyle loved the festive vibe. People were spray-painting silly, political, profane, absurd, loving statements everywhere.

Even when having fun, the black cloud of the pandemic wasn't far away.

Two people he knew died of the disease, both in the prime of life. He was taking all the prescribed precautions, with hand sanitizers "everywhere" and masking. But he didn't find himself thinking of "life and death" issues more often.

"I am self-employed," he said, "so I have had concerns about government restrictions in the beginning, by trying to shut things down and stifle us. That has been a concern of mine."

He was an entrepreneur and in charge of keeping his employees safe.

"In my place of business," he said, "we've taken precautions. We help and protect employees. If someone has a concern, we allow them to distance in whatever manner they feel necessary."

As for masking, he didn't wear them all the time, but he's not an "anti-masker." The family Christmas and Thanksgiving were scaled back.

"I think people can be somewhat responsible on their own," he said. "Across the street here we can see people masking and some without, but most of them are socially distancing."

Overall, he does "have a problem with government overreaching on things.

"I'd like to see the government let us move on," he said. "I do believe that people are taking it seriously."

His family was coming back from a long ski vacation to Colorado. He said many facilities there were closed, but people were mostly masking and distancing.

"It was a change, but it wasn't a significant change (from last year's ski vacation)," he said. "We still had fun. We visited with friends we have in Colorado. But at the same time, there was a little bit of a distancing there. There was no hugging involved. No handshaking. The occasional fist bump."

He thought the mindset had shifted on personal contact between people. He feared people may never go back to the way things were.

"I'm a personal contact person, I like personal contact," he said. "I'll put my arm around a friend's neck or shake hands. I like that sort of thing. That has been a little bit of a hindrance to me, but not major."

He worried about his four school-aged children The pandemic put restrictions on their school, church, and Cub Scout interactions.

"It's been tougher for my children than it has been for us," he said. "The social interaction at school, they enjoy that. And with that being taken away from them, that's been tough. Not just with outside groups but with youth church activities. Even something as simple as … Cubs Scouts. And with limitations on that - and being involved with other people - it has been tougher on my children than it has been for us."

It was the day before Easter, and I asked how it changed his Easter plans.

"We kinda made the choice to be on the road for Easter," he said, "because we knew we weren't going to be at home having a large gathering."

"Everybody is Missing Everybody"

ASKED if they are spending more time together in the first year of the pandemic, Linda Lyle laughed at the question.

"Oh, definitely," she said, laughing at the understatement.

Later in the interview, she teared up when she thought of all the people she loves but couldn't spend more time with.

Linda and Douglas Lyle were at the Cadillac Ranch, outside Amarillo. It's a roadside art exhibit featuring tail-in-the-air Cadillacs in a cow field. It's a popular surreal exhibit in a cow pasture along Route 66.

They hadn't seen their family for a year and a half. No family gatherings on Thanksgiving, birthdays or marriages.

Douglas's oil and gas job required quarantining. Any visit to their families in Canada would have taken two weeks before and after the visit. They couldn't take five weeks off.

Both natives of Ottawa, they moved to Midland, Texas shortly before the pandemic hit.

"So we didn't get out to meet any local people," she said.

No family. No friends. Just FaceTime, and each other.

"We try to make the best out of it, but, yes, it is hard," she said. "We miss our family. And when we're talking to our family members and they're crying ... everybody is missing everybody."

Linda visibly choked up, tears well up in her eyes.

On a scale of 1 to 10, with 1 being the worst year, Linda said it "probably" was the worst year.

Did they think there were more years like this ahead?

"I think the past government really made a real mess of this," she said. "I think now we're a little better off."

Douglas pointed out that the governments of Canada, the USA, and the State of Texas each had very different responses.

"The city of Midland, where we live, is terrible," said Linda, saying she stayed away from restaurants where locals go unmasked. "The people do not want to wear masks. People don't want to social distance. People are just fighting it the whole way."

The "buy-in" was good at the beginning, Douglas said, but it quickly faded.

The couple limited the number of times they went for groceries, and they bundled errands. They did it for their health but mainly for the health of everybody they met.

"If you're sick, you don't go out," said Douglas, adding that it was the way they were raised. "We don't want to infect people unknowingly. With this disease, you might not know if you have it because it's asymptomatic. So how do you know that?"

Some people don't know how to respond.

"It's something, as a society, we haven't had to deal with before," Douglas said. "So how people are responding is based on what they know. And a lack of trust in what the government is telling them."

I asked which government they listen to, and Linda Douglas said, "Dr. Fauci."

As for the future, Douglas pointed to death statistics showing the "virus was still rampant."

"The more people it infects, the more chances it has to mutate," he said. "I think I trust the science."

They were unmasked outside and came north from Midland to go to the giant 180-foot white cross in Groom, another Route 66 landmark site. They were going to an outdoor Stations of the Cross for Easter, a Christian ritual reenacting the crucifixion day of Jesus.

They spent their Route 66 pandemic Easter on the Way of Sorrows.

Road Tripper Vows to Fight Pandemics

THE PANDEMIC BOUNCED Kevin Horn out of the Peace Corps in Madagascar, but it gave him a new life mission.

When I met him at the Cadillac Ranch, he was headed to Johns Hopkins in the fall to become a scientist with lofty dreams. I asked what he wanted to major in.

"Hopefully, helping out in these Covid times," he said. "Try to create a medical device that could maybe prevent infection."

The Peace Corps evacuated 7,200 Peace Corps volunteers across the world in 2020. Horn returned and helped at the local Red Cross before applying to graduate schools.

He enrolled in Johns Hopkins' doctorate program in material science and engineering. He aimed to specialize in biomaterials.

The "ranch" features ten Cadillac cars submerged at the hood, tailgates in the air. It's the #1 roadside attraction along Route 66, just outside Amarillo.

Before starting school in the fall, he was road-tripping to "all the national parks ... across America." After this, he was on his way to Texas's Big Bend National Park.

"I hope that everyone gets vaccinated and that everyone masks up ... (for) the last few months of Covid, that's all I ask," he said.

I asked how the pandemic affected his social relationships and happiness.

"It's been tough, all these Zoom meetings and meeting people virtually, it just doesn't compare," he said. "I'm really looking forward to meeting my friends back in person, sharing a board game, or like, having dinner with friends once we're all vaccinated."

He was in his 20s, healthy, and wearing a mask outside. I asked him if this behavior was going to be the new normal. He thought the pandemic might be weakening by as early as fall, 2021.

"For Covid, it seems to be a seasonal thing because the coronavirus is just a rapidly evolving class of viruses," he said. "It may change every year like the flu, so we'll have to wait and see on those results."

We may end up masking like the Japanese do, he said, particularly if a person is sick or older.

As he was being interviewed, a woman photo-bombed him from behind.

"Trump 2024," she said as she walked by.

"Fuck Trump," he said over his shoulder, on camera.

It was an on-camera example of how divided the country was after the January 6th storming of the Capitol Building in Washington, DC.

The Cadillac Ranch supplies free spray paint cans for self-expression throughout the ranch. People paint on the cars and some on the cow field pathway. Messages of love, silliness, politics, and, sometimes, hate are temporarily written on the land.

Before the interview, Horn crossed out a pro-Trump message on the cow path pathway dirt. It was seen as offensive to the Trump supporter.

Although Horn got the last word in on the video, the unmasked woman returned later red-faced and highly agitated. She angrily berated him before walking off to her vehicle parked beside Route 66.

He appeared surprised at her in-your-face anger and made his way back to Route 66 too.

Surreal ranch. Surreal politics. Surreal Pandemic.

Space Force Son & Art Teacher Dad Talk Covid

VISITING the Cadillac Ranch on their way home to New Mexico, the Lutz family gave their opinions on how the pandemic was going on both sides of the Atlantic Ocean.

The father, Anthony Lutz, was still living in Rio Rancho, New Mexico. His son Jacob Lutz was visiting from England, where he worked for Space Force, one of eight US military services.

Anthony Lutz was a high school art teacher in New Mexico struggling with teaching art, both online and in person.

"It's a great challenge," Anthony Lutz said. "Overall, some are doing extremely well and others are failing miserably."

Some of his students and extended family contracted the disease. Anthony Lutz had a mild flu but wasn't tested for Covid. The rest of his immediate family was Covid-free.

Anniversaries, holidays, and even his son's wedding had to be shifted due to pandemic concerns. Lutz was concerned about personal interactions during the pandemic.

He appreciated more time with his wife at home, but work was more stressful.

"One thing I don't like," he said, "we haven't been interacting well as human beings. I'm seeing less and less personal interaction, just saying hello. People don't even want to say hello to you. I think it's awkward in a lot of ways. It's been difficult."

On the positive side, he said the pandemic provided more time at home with the family.

"In other ways, it's been great," he said. "As I said, we've spent more time together, and that's been fantastic."

Wearing a NASA T-shirt, Jacob Lutz and his new wife were living in the United Kingdom for the last six months.

"Things were a lot more locked down than in the United States," he said.

He said both he and his wife were struggling to "make friends."

It was the day before Easter, and Jacob Lutz said he planned to go to services.

"Something that I believe in is that the Bible encourages people to gather together in fellowship. And that's really challenging when you have a society that says we need to not gather, we need to not be together. My personal belief is that's not how God has designed humans to operate."

As for Jacob Lutz's happiness, he admitted the pandemic made the adjustment "tough."

"For several months, it definitely affected my wife because it was difficult for her to get out and really do anything," he said. "It made it harder for her to go out and get a job, so she doesn't have a job. It disrupted her (nurse) schooling. She's been stuck at home, without a lot of options to get out and socialize and see England. She'd never been there before. It's definitely been hard on the both of us."

I asked both how they thought the government was responding to the crisis.

"Definitely, at the beginning, I think it was good to be cautious because none of us knew what we were dealing with, so I was willing to play along," Anthony Lutz said. "But as things start coming out more and more, we're finding that certain groups of people are having trouble with it and other types of people are not. I think in our state in particular, it's been a challenge getting the vaccines to the ones who really need it."

Prior to the pandemic, Anthony Lutz believed "the media." The pandemic reporting changed his mind.

"There's a lot of spin," Anthony Lutz said. "It's difficult to know who is telling me the truth and what their motivations are.

"I don't like to be at that place in life where you're questioning everything, You're telling me the truth as best as you know it. And I want to tell my son the best that I can possibly know it. And I don't want politics (involved). I think it's getting really muddy right now."

Jacob Lutz was vaccinated due to his military service, and he was "hoping as they (vaccines) roll out we'll go back to seeing a lot more people used to being back together again ... I think that's how society needs to work."

Anthony Lutz chimed in.

"We need to connect to each other. There's a lot of things separating us from each other. I think that doing meetings and stuff like that online, it's not as creative. You don't get the answers that you need or get to the answers as fast. We need to be able to interact with people in order to solve problems."

Anthony Lutz said he "knows Covid is real" because even if the total number of dead is off by half, "there are still more people dying ... I'm not one of those deniers."

When the interview ended, Anthony Lutz wanted to interview me about my religion and "faith."

I said I don't talk politics or religion. I also never give my pandemic opinions.

My non-answer prompted Anthony Lutz to hand me a pocket-sized red card.

"Love God and Love Others."

Fatalism and God at Love's

BETHARD RAY LAWSON was on his way home from a California road trip on Route 66 when I caught up with him at a Love's truck stop outside Amarillo.

A resident of West Memphis, Arkansas, he had friends and family who contracted Covid and recovered. However, he was Covid-free, and he thought the pandemic was being overblown.

"I know it's real because I've had it in my family," he said. "But I think the press has over-politicized it, and the government."

He approached the pandemic with religious fatalism.

"I'm a child of God," he said. "I believe the hairs on your head and the hairs on my head are numbered. Each and every one of them. If it's my day to go ... if it's your day to go, ain't no doctor that can save you ... On the flip side of that, if it's not your time to go, sir, there ain't nothing you can catch that's going to take you."

His fate during the pandemic was determined before he was born. "I believe," he said, "it's all planned out."

He occasionally wore a cover over his mouth for other people's protection, "not mine." All you need to know is on his wristband.

"Personally, I don't stress, I don't worry about anything because I know, as this wristband says, 'God is Big Enough.'" he said. "He's big enough to take care of anything. You can ask him, and he will."

He worried about the left-leaning press. He said, "It's hard to believe the press," when it comes to the pandemic.

Pandemic policies on the border also worried him. He believed migrants were being let into America without testing for Covid (a claim found to be mostly untrue).

"If Covid is such a big problem as the news projects it to be, why are they doing that, why is the government allowing that to happen?" he said. "That's how I feel about it."

He supported "choice" in mask-wearing and pointed out that Texas had no mask mandate at the time. He believed "the government is taking too much control of things. Period."

He was a staunch proponent of individualism.

"I believe you're smart enough to know what your family needs," he said. "You don't need the government to say, 'Oh, you can't have your business open. We don't want (people) coming in there.' That's not their job. Their job is to protect the country. ... Need I say any more?"

Life's a 10 with Family & Altruism

AT A LOVE'S Truck Stop outside of Amarillo, Aaron Eskam looked like any other young father on a family vacation. There were no outward signs that he was also one of the happiest.

"I have a wife and five kids," he said. "We homeschool our kids, so they were already remote learning from the start. I work in tech, so we went all remote as a company. So there's no real impact there either. It's a pretty quick transition because I'm always working on a computer anyway."

Some might think that having everyone home at once is a burden - not Eskam. His key to happiness in pandemic times was a mix of concern for others and a love of the home life.

"For us, definitely, it's been great having more time as a family," he said. "I can go eat lunch with the wife and the kids, and we can walk during the middle of the day. I get to be out in the sun a bit more during the day, instead of always coming home after dark. It's been pretty good for us."

One of the reasons they are so strict about isolating themselves was so they could feel comfortable about visiting elderly family members. His family was enjoying the change in lifestyle.

"For us, it's been great," he said. "We lived in Norman (Oklahoma) because that's where the job was, but now if we want to locate somewhere else, that's an option."

Then he blew me away with the most pro-pandemic experience of the trip. I asked on a scale of 1 to 10, with 10 being the happiest, how happy he was during the pandemic.

"In terms of just general happiness," he said, "my family is everything. So the more time I get to spend with them, the better. So I think we're probably around a 10. In terms of general dynamics. Of course, we're not excited about Covid in general."

As for the government's response to the pandemic, Eskam gave a nuanced response. Local, state, and federal responses have differed. He finds different rules every time he "stops for gas" on his trip from Oklahoma to Colorado.

He saw an article about Republican versus Democrat state responses to the pandemic, and the "information wasn't that conclusive." His impression was that "we'll transition" out of the masks in six months to a year.

He thought "the American personality" won't allow masking

forever. He's seen a lot of fighting over mask use. As for now, he was focused on wearing a mask "to protect people around me."

"It's maybe," he said, "thinking about other people a little bit more instead of just, 'Is it going to protect me personally?' And you can debate science on that some, but show some consideration for other people."

"Real suffering isn't just about physical pain, but about not knowing when the pain will end, not knowing what the point of it all is."
— Albuquerque-native Kirstin Valdez Quade, author of The Five Wounds.

"The combination of song, prayer, and poetry is a natural form of expression for many Navajo people. A person who is able to "talk beautifully" is well thought of and considered wealthy."
— Luci Tapahonso, the first poet laureate of the Navajo Nation.

THE GREAT DIVIDES

NEW MEXICO

*T*he Pequod broke down in Illinois, Missouri, Oklahoma, and twice in New Mexico.

Riding on a bicycle at risk of catastrophic breakdowns felt symbolic of the pandemic dynamic. Uncertainty in motion.

About 80 miles outside Albuquerque, I noticed my back tire was wobbling more with each mile. Too far to walk. I had to keep riding. I rode over a 7,000-foot pass and through the Sandia-Manzano mountains to Albuquerque, not knowing if the next downstroke was the last.

After being fixed in Albuquerque, the Pequod broke down again outside of town, so I returned for an overhaul. From Albuquerque onward, bicycle shops were spaced hundreds of miles apart.

That first night out of Albuquerque, I rode past small Laguna Pueblo communities with "No Visitors Allowed" signs blocking the entrances. The quarantined Indian communities looked like locked-down camps.

Route 66 passes through or near ten Indian pueblos in New Mexico.

New Mexico has the largest percentage of Hispanic and Latino Americans and the second highest percentage, after Alaska, of Native

Americans. It's a majority-minority state, one of six in the US, with less than 50 percent non-Hispanic Whites.

It's also one of the poorest states in the country, with more than 18 percent of its people living below the poverty line. Government and related jobs dominate the job market, along with finance, real estate, insurance, and rentals. Mining, gas/oil, and quarry are the largest contributors to the GDP.

I rode the length of the state through San Jon, Tucumcari, Montoya, Newkirk, Santa Rosa, Clines Corner, Moriarty, Tijeras, Albuquerque, Paraje, McCarthys, and Grants and over the Great Divide in the Zumi Mountains, Ramah, Vanderwagen, and Gallup.

I crossed the Continental Divide on a snowy, freezing day. The mountains were white with snowflakes that drifted lightly in the air. I was wandering in a snow globe.

My GPS stopped working when I rode over the rugged local roads near the Great Divide so I relied on dead reckoning. The mountain roads were as silent as the wind.

It was authentic solo riding, seeing how isolated people live up there.

I finally found my way off the Great Divide and onto I-40. The interstate replaces Historic Route 66 for long stretches in New Mexico and Arizona. So I rode along interstate shoulders with trucks and cars passing me like harpoons meant for me.

Coming off the Great Divide, I rode into the Colorado Plateau, with the country's greatest concentration of national parks. The plateau spans Colorado, Utah, and the rest of Route 66 until I left Arizona.

Out in the open spaces, I saw wild horses grazing and running in herds. The first horses were brought over by ship to Mexico by the Spanish conquistador Hernan Cortes in 1519.

On the Route 66 road shoulder outside Gallup, I stopped for a moment to examine a dead horse.

The horse's blood was dry, so I guessed it had died violently earlier that day. The horse was lying on its side as if posing mid-gallop toward freedom.

I saw a variety of roadkill during the trip, including a dead porcupine, a wild boar, two dogs, two deer, and many birds.

Interaction with people on the move killed those animals. Interspecies interaction is also the source of most pandemics. Bats, rats, monkeys, and wild waterfowl were the source of most pandemics.

Outside of Albuquerque, I saw the New Mexico state bird dash across the road, a real roadrunner. It bolted across all lanes and vanished from my view.

Roadrunners among the Hopi and Ancestral Puebloans in New Mexico were medicinal birds warding off evil spirits, aka diseases.

The roadrunner's power over life and death was so strong that it led to disagreements.

Some believed roadrunners were sacred and key to keeping humans safe from disease. Others thought eating the sacred roadrunner gave a person strength and boosted "immunity."

Native Americans believed in interspecies transfers of health and immunity, but they couldn't agree on the right medicine. To eat the roadrunner or worship the roadrunner. It was a choice as real to them and a choice of vaccinate or not.

I thought of the Great Divide and all that separates people, like politics, race, intelligence, wealth, and status. It struck me as I rode the greatest divide of all is between the sick and the well.

Drifter Gave Free Food Away in Mexico

BOB WILLIAMS WAS STRANDED at Russell's Travel Stop at the border of Texas and New Mexico.

His yellow school bus broke down west of there on I-40. He needed to hitchhike back to the bus with containers of motor oil and his dog.

"Hey, where are you going?" he kept asking people as they walked into the travel center. "Hey, where are YOU going?"

It was the wrong question to ask. He was getting no help, and many people seemed threatened by him.

He described himself as being "a traveling man ... for a long time."

Rochester, New York, was his hometown, but he was really from "the corner of bedlam and squalor." It was a reference to a quip by musician Tom Waits.

Williams was a free spirit drifter on his way to California. It was just him, his dog and the bus. After he California, he was headed "all over."

I asked how he spent his pandemic year and the told a surprising story of generosity on the road.

He and his girlfriend were nearly broke, but they had kitchen equipment. They ran a street food business in New Mexico that went belly up when the pandemic hit. Events began shutting down, and they were out of business.

So they started a GoFundMe crowd-sourcing page, bought food, and drove their gear south to the Pacific Coast of Mexico, to San Blas, Nayrit, three hours north of Puerto Vallarta.

The tiny community was "impoverished" by the pandemic shutdowns.

"We felt like we were part of the community, and we should do something," he said, "so we did."

They set up their equipment in the back of a bar shuttered by the pandemic. The owner was a friend of theirs. They made pork and egg sandwiches there, wrapped them up, and gave them away on the streets.

"I'd wake up, do breakfast, like 80 to 100 meals a day, where it was just me and her (his girlfriend)," he said. "I'd cook 'em all up. Put them in the aluminum foil - whatever it was, a pulled pork sandwich - American-style, with some coleslaw, some greens. Sometimes it was Mexican - tortillas and eggs - huevos rancheros ... It was a dirt road kinda town. It was hot. It was sweaty. But it was worth it. It was cool."

For about "a month and a half," they gave food away.

As for the pandemic back in the states, he masked and distanced depending on the circumstances.

"If I was in a restaurant and there were more older people, I'd probably mask up for their sake," he said. "But I'm a young buck. And if I'm around ... people who aren't really in the bracket of people getting hurt, extreme Covid, if you want to call it that (then no mask)."

I asked if the government acted properly during the pandemic, and he laughed. The government "acting properly" was "an oxymoron."

Everything's always political, he said, and always will be. Governments act "for themselves," and it's up to people to decide how to live with that. They can "play chess with that" or "join the rat race and be part of their system."

Or people could be more like him and "be a recluse and break down on a bus down the road and just be a lonesome, lonely boy."

President Joe Biden's election would probably cool down the politics of a pandemic, he hoped. But Biden wasn't going to get him to vaccinate.

"I think I've had hangovers that would stand up to the Covid virus," he said. "But I might be wrong and on a ventilator and wanting to retract that statement ... If it's not Covid, it's going to be this, it's going to be that, it's going to be cancer. It's on your shoulder, and it's coming for you, it's coming for us."

He had advice for all Americans during pandemic times.

"Just enjoy the time you have," he said. "Do what you can to not make waves. Do what you can to protect your family.

"But don't go overboard. You don't have to go get an assault rifle and a no-mask-fucking-Trump-sticker, or whatever, just to be a hard-ass. Like protection? No, that's insecurity ... Be secure enough to come have a conversation with a stranger. Help out a stranger."

When I mentioned it was Easter, he smiled with a Magic Bus/Merry Prankster smile and said, "I thought it was April Fools."

When the interview was finished, I helped him find a ride. He was asking for rides all the wrong way. I've done some hitchhiking in my day, so I took over.

I asked people for him. I used the good Samaritan sales pitch. This guy is stranded. Can you help out a person in need? It worked on the second try. He'd been there a long time. I smiled smugly.

He picked up his two containers of motor oil, called for his dog, and rode away on I-40 with a young woman who was herself moving out West.

I slept at the back of the Russell's Travel Center parking lot. The next morning, I rode a few miles west on the two-lane Historic Route 66 and saw him beside the interstate, inside a broken-down yellow school bus with a wooden door.

I shouted at him and waived from around 50 yards away.

He was on his cell phone, presumably calling for help from the emergency shoulder of I-40. He stuck his head out and waved from the rear emergency exit door.

I waved back and kept riding past another iconic Route 66 scene, a drifter in a broken-down bus rolling nowhere.

As I rode, it dawned on me that I'd just seen the corner of bedlam and squalor.

Couple Quarantines in Separate Houses

FOR THE DRISKILLS, the pandemic really hit homes.

In order to quarantine properly, they decided they must quarantine themselves from each other.

The Driskills owned two homes side by side, so Catherine Driskill and her daughter stayed in one house, and her husband moved into the other.

Her husband's job made quarantining impossible, so Catherine and her daughter were on their own from March until the fall of 2020.

"I didn't see him for six months," she said. "I put his food out on the porch, and I'd call him and say, 'Your food's okay.' And he'd come and get his food. And he'd wave to me through the glass."

I met her at Russell's Travel Center along Route 66, near the Texas/New Mexico border.

She was driving her daughter to Chandler, Oklahoma, to live with her biological father "because she wants to live in the big city."

Catherine Driskill's quarantine was a bit less restrictive due to the family's 11.5 acres near Paintsville, Kentucky.

"That was our saving grace, we don't live in the city," she said. "I had lots of books. I took some internet classes ... I got a lot done. I worked on the house. Worked on the property."

She didn't believe masks have real medical value, but she masked up for the sake of other people.

"They (masks) make people feel better," she said. "So we're supposed to be kind. So I figure, if it makes people feel better, I'll wear a mask. Since it's no big deal."

Her husband taught at a university and was required to get a vaccine. He chose the Johnson & Johnson vaccine "because we want to avoid the Pfizer and Moderna."

She did not want to get a vaccine at all.

"If I have to get a vaccine, I'll get the Johnson & Johnson, but I'd just as soon not," she said. "I have lots of allergies, and I don't trust them."

She believed that the government will attempt to prolong pandemic restrictions in a bid to control Americans.

"I think that the powers that be have had a taste of absolute power," she said, "and it's going to take some reeling back to get them to stop putting that much control over people."

Maybe because she didn't believe the US government had good motives during the pandemic, she didn't believe Covid was killing people any faster than the seasonal flu.

"I think they're going to be using this (pandemic) for purposes that they don't need to be using it for," she said. "The death rates for Covid are about the same as for the flu. So we don't do this for the flu. There's no need to do this for Covid. But unfortunately, people die. People die from the flu. It looks like Covid is going to be here from now on out, so we may as well get used to it."

Anti-Vax Conspiracies of a Covid Team Worker

SHERRI GOEN BROUGHT a picnic for her children to the playground across from the Albuquerque Zoo. Her daughter was in her arms, fidgeting and coughing.

"I do work in the medical field," she said. "I work on what is called 'The Covid Team' for Sandia National Labs in Albuquerque."

Neither she nor her four children contracted the disease. She socially distanced from family and friends "most of the time" but sometimes "goes visit."

Despite being a certified medical assistant for a Covid Team, she wasn't vaccinated.

"I am not vaccinated. I don't feel the need," she said. "Since I've been healthy this whole time. My kids have stayed healthy. So I don't think it's a need for me or any of my children to get vaccinated."

She heard "bad" stories and worried more about the vaccine than the virus.

"I just don't want to put that kinda stuff in my body right now," she said. "I've heard a lot of stories about it. There's been people who've come through it just fine. And there's people, things have happened to them. They've gotten sicker. Put in the hospital. Or passed away. I just really don't want to take a chance. It doesn't sound healthy."

She worried that the US government was part of the problem during the epidemic.

"My personal feelings are that the government has caused a lot of this," she said. "Honestly, I don't know that for a fact. I just feel that could be possible with everything that's going on with how quick the Covid came in to play with everybody."

She "feels like" the government deliberately caused Covid "because there are a certain amount of numbers they need to reduce."

Specifically, she thought the government was killing off the poor.

"Lower income families that aren't really helping society as much as they can because they are so low on the totem pole," she said. "I feel like (the government) kinda did it, to do a kinda wash out, basically."

The government, she believed, was controlling our lives and wanted to get rid of certain people.

"I just know how much control the government has over people and society," she said. "They have so much control over everyone through so many different things. Through your television. Your phones. Through the news. They have so much control."

Most people, she said, don't know they are being manipulated.

"And I feel like on that note, people watch the news so closely that it affects them terminally. Because everything that is being broadcasted out through there, it gets to people's brains. And the majority of people in life do not know how to control their emotions and how they perceive things. They don't really know how to control all that."

She believed the government takeover was leading to suicides.

"So the government has an advantage right there," she said. "It's easy for them to just take over. And I've heard throughout the last year or so that people have actually taken their lives because of it. Not anybody personal that I know, but people, you know, in the US and outside of the US because they get so depressed with everything going on."

Her personal life improved during the pandemic's first year. She moved back from Florida, switched to a better-paying job, and was taking classes to get her real estate license. She was keeping safe, she said, by living right.

"I'm just happy that I'm healthy through the whole pandemic," she said. "Thankful to vitamins and healthy eating.

High Anxiety at a Family Picnic

CARLOS GRIEGO WAS out with his wife and toddler for a "duck feeding and hot dog day."

I veered to the side of the road when I saw the Griegos gathered around a wooden picnic table in a tiny Albuquerque city roadside park by 8th Street and Central Avenue.

From the road, they looked like an idyllic picture of urban family fun. Their 16-month-old son was full of mischief. And the hot dogs were going down fast.

Griego held his son on his lap and sipped on his soft drink. He appeared casual and cool as he spoke about his consuming pandemic anxiety.

Griego felt like the enemy had him surrounded. The unseen, ubiquitous nature of an airborne virus was getting to him.

"Covid is all around you," he said, "just waiting for you to be touched by it."

The pandemic had already infected two of his daughters, several friends, and his wife's family members. He lived in a household with five people, and he worried for the safety of each one of them. His mother was at high risk because she was a double lung transplant survivor.

"Covid has definitely run amok around people that we know and where we live," he said.

His family was "super vigilant" with masks, hand sanitizers, social distancing, and staying away from restaurants and parties.

Precautions were the result of his anxiety, he said, not the end of his anxiety.

"I'm already an anxious person," he said. "I suffer from anxiety."

Griego was shot in 2003 and has suffered post-traumatic stress syndrome ever since. The pandemic "heightened that" angst.

The pandemic threatens livelihoods and health, he said, and that's what most people worry about.

"Two of the main components that humans constantly worry about - Covid or not Covid - are finances and health," he said. "Even if you weren't a naturally anxious person prior to Covid, I think you probably have developed some kind of anxiety ... For me, I find myself pretty much functioning at a high anxiety level daily."

He compared it to life-and-death thoughts soldiers deal with in combat. For him, the pandemic exacerbated feelings of mortal uncertainty during everyday life.

"Now I think civilians have been impacted, and their anxiety levels have gone through the roof because of this," he said. "There are some people who have lost their jobs. Lost their homes. Lost people who were close to them. Some people who were healthy that died. So the uncertainty of the disease is what gives everybody some sort of anxiety."

He cited a rap song by the rapper DMX, who died earlier that weekend. The rap told people to slow down and appreciate life.

Griego noted that the United States posted by far more pandemic deaths than any other country, proving in his mind that the US government did not handle it well.

"We are still talking about three or four or fifth waves, like, we can't get it under control," he said. "We just came from feeding the ducks. There were probably 200 people there with no masks."

He believed the pandemic was going to have a long horizon.

"I'm going to be less open to going to a concert," he said. "Even if we get Covid in check, who's to say there isn't another pandemic around the corner?"

Nevertheless, he saw some good that could come from people adapting to the new realities of life. An environmental compliance worker with gas stations, he used to be on the road more. Since the pandemic hit, he was able to work from home for most of his young son's life.

"It literally comes down to taking care of you and your family," he said. "And appreciating life and appreciating what we have because if we haven't taken anything else away from this Covid situation, it's that life is precious. And the people who were doing fine a year and a half ago, there's a half million of them dead right now, if not more."

The pandemic reminds us, he thought, of what's important in life.

"It's a blessing in a sense because you learn to take life in stride, and slow down and just kinda enjoy it," he said.

However, those thoughts don't make the existential dread go away.

"I think," he said, "people will be dealing with the anxieties of this for at least decades."

Mothers against Pandemic

Susan Cruthers and Angel Garcia talked about a pandemic-safe senior graduation party as they sat around an outdoor table at Whole Foods in Albuquerque.

They were thinking of having people coming in shifts to the party, so the crowd wouldn't get too big. Ten people per shift seemed a safe number.

They both had family, friends, and co-workers who contracted Covid. Garcia's son's piano teacher died.

"There've been times when I have been anxious, and I haven't been able to sleep, just worrying about ... not just about us, but worrying about the whole community and the whole country," Cruthers said.

Garcia was reaching out to friends to make sure they were well.

"I've still tried to text people to make sure they're okay ... (and) call people to make sure they're okay," Garcia said.

The pandemic changed her, Cruthers said.

"I've learned not to rush around so much," Cruthers said. "Be a little more satisfied at home. And connecting with the people closest to you."

On the good side, the pandemic allowed them to be closer to their sons during a key year in their lives.

"Having seniors, they've been at home," Garcia said. "And spending more time with them, I think, has been a great benefit because they are leaving the nest soon."

Garcia joked that her husband still worked outside the home, which she laughingly said was good for her marriage. Cruthers said her husband was working at home.

They both liked what the state is doing about the vaccine rollout, saying Gov. Michelle Lujan Grisham was "proactive." Cruthers thought the national response under President Trump was "a disaster."

"You're never going to be 100 percent happy with anything, we've learned, but I think she did do a great job (rolling out vaccines)," Garcia said. "Right now, New Mexico is #1 in getting the vaccine out and getting it to the rural communities. So I'm not going to like everything, but for the most part, we've been safe. So I'm pretty happy about it."

Going forward, they thought masks might be a "winter accessory," and more variants may be popping up in the future.

"We'll have to wait and see," Garcia said.

"There's definitely silver linings to it"

LUCAS ELLIOTT WAS an accountant being photo-bombed by his wife and child as he talked outside ABQ BioPark Zoo.

"I've actually been pretty lucky (during Covid)," he said. "I've been able to work from home the entire time, so in a lot of ways, it's made work easier for me."

A resident of Albuquerque, he loved spending time with his young son while remote working.

"I would spend 12 hours out of the house on a workday," he said. "I get to spend more time with my kid than I would otherwise. There's definitely silver linings to it."

His father, however, lived in Spain. Travel was impossible at the time. His father hadn't seen his son yet. His wife's family was also "all over the country," so it was difficult to "hang out" with the extended family.

He and his wife were vaccinated, distancing and masking, "so the anxiety I had is relieved by that."

"I mostly take the recommended precautions, and we mostly stay around our own bubble for the most part," he said. "After a year, it's hard not to want to socialize and get in groups."

The government response, he thought, started out slow, and morphed into politics. On the other hand, the vaccine rollout was "a pretty good job."

"I think, probably, in the beginning, there could have been a more focused response," he said. "It just seems like it became a political statement about whether or not you were going to wear a mask in a crowd. And it took on a meaning it probably shouldn't have. On the other hand, I think we did a pretty good job with rolling out vaccinations."

He longed for the day when a "critical mass" of vaccinated people will spell the end of the pandemic. Or the return to a more normal existence as soon as possible.

"Maybe by the end of summer," he said, "we'll get back to normal."

He did not believe Covid significantly changed the way he thinks about life, except that he was grateful for silver linings.

"I don't think it made me all that much more introspective," he said. "I guess I'm grateful that if I was going to live through a global pandemic, it happened during the first year of my kid's life. I sorta got to spend more time with him than I would have otherwise."

"The Pit" & Nature's Population Control

To INCREASE his chances of surviving Covid, Ken Krause got in line at "The Pit."

At 79 years old, Ken Krause knew his age put him at a higher risk so he joined thousands of people lined up for a shot at Albuquerque's mass vaccination center, the University of New Mexico's sports arena.

Informally known as The Pit, it is so named because the playing floor is 37 feet below ground level. The Pit has a capacity of 15,411 people.

Krause stood in line twice for shots and "enjoyed it."

During our lunch at the Frontier restaurant in Albuquerque, he talked about masking and distancing.

"I don't know too many people who have had Covid," he said. "I've been distancing. Been washing my own dishes. Cooking my own meals."

He hasn't been getting together with friends as often. He plays golf if he can.

Three friends died of non-Covid causes, but he couldn't attend their funerals because of pandemic precautions. Some services were scheduled for the summer. One friend had a virtual funeral.

"The funeral was on the internet," he said.

He found himself alone more often. He didn't think his lifestyle changes were dramatic or tragic.

"Uneventful, to me, this year, Covid," he said.

Being vaccinated and taking precautions, he wasn't worried about the pandemic taking him.

"I heard something about my blood type," he said. "I'm a type O. I've been healthy all my life. I've done a lot of crazy things and all that. But that, I think, had something to do about it. I heard on the news that people with type O blood were less likely to get the virus."

Then he veered away from his personal experience to his views on evolution. He thought the pandemic might have a corrective evolutionary function.

"It seems like so many people in the world now, we're overcrowded, I think," he said. "And this is something like cleaning up things, I don't know ... making the population a little bit lesser so we don't have these things. It's like animals ... if they're together too much and there's an overabundance of the same breed, they disease themselves, and then they'll die off, and one day all of them will die off."

He compared the pandemic deaths to the culling of the deer in Wisconsin.

"The deer population in Wisconsin, we have a hunting season because they don't want the deer population to get too big," he said. "Because they hang out together, and they inter-breed, and all that. It's the same way with humans, I imagine. We're animals, in a sense too."

The pandemic might be nature's way of culling the human herd, he speculated.

"God and nature," he said.

"My happiness level has gone up"

I FEARED BEING STUCK WAITING for bicycle repairs or a new wheel in Albuquerque.

The distances between towns in the Western United States made bicycle breakdowns more dangerous and challenging. Bicycle shops can be 300 to 400 miles apart.

The first bicycle shop I brought my bicycle to in Albuquerque did not allow customers inside the shop due to Covid precautions.

An employee came outside, diagnosed the problem, and then brought the bicycle inside to be fixed. I needed three spokes, and the wobbly back wheel needed to be trued.

The next day, it broke down again about 25 miles outside of Albuquerque. I rode back to the same shop, and the bicycle mechanic threw up his hands, saying it might take him weeks to schedule another repair.

So I rode to The Bike Coop in one last-ditch effort to save my bicycle and the trip.

The owner and mechanics stood around my bicycle like doctors around a Covid patient on life support.

During the pandemic, new bicycles often took months or better to buy. I bought my 40-year-old bicycle on Craigslist from a Polish immigrant back in Chicago.

Bicycle parts were tough to order. Neither Albuquerque bicycle shop had a new wheel in stock. The Bike Coop worried they didn't have the proper spokes or time to rebuild the wheel.

They found a way, and Amanda Batty even gave an interview about her experiences during the pandemic.

Originally from Utah, Batty said they made an "emergency

exception" for Pequod. The shop was "drowning" in work, but they saw a rider in need of emergency assistance.

"We kinda gave up on getting new bikes," she said. "We're building up bikes."

She'd been working 17 days without a day off.

"Yep, and before that, it was 42, and before that, it was about 74," she said, laughing under her mask.

She had not contracted Covid, but another mechanic in the shop did. Many of her family and friends caught it.

"We have 500,000 Americans who've died from it. Everybody knows someone who's had it."

The pandemic struck some communities in the Albuquerque area harder than others.

"I've already gotten the vaccine," she said. "Everybody here (in the shop) has. We're incredibly fortunate to have gotten it. It's a pandemic that has severely affected the Navajo Nation here."

She wished the vaccine had rolled out earlier and more could have been done to help those in need.

Many small Albuquerque businesses closed, and some may never come back. However, the demand created by Covid was good for the cycling world.

"A lot of amazing things have happened in this last year," she said, adding The Bike Coop was giving bikes and free repairs to underprivileged families.

She felt "happy" during the pandemic.

"My anxiety level, I would say, has gone down," she said. "My happiness level has gone up. Then again, I'm a hermit. So it hasn't been all negative for me."

Her almost evangelical outlook on how bicycles can change the world swept me away.

"I think that a lot of people who got on bikes this past year are going to stay on bikes. And I think we've also managed to adopt millions of new missionaries, if you will, toward the cycling cause.

"A lot of people estimated it would slow down, but when you have millions and millions and millions of people who, all around the globe, have gotten on bikes, it's not going to disappear. It's not a temporary thing. Certainly not when bikes are such an incredible vehicle for so much growth and progress. That's not a small impact. And I think we're going to see it for decades and generations to come."

"Have empathy and compassion"

Albuquerque police officer Hence Williams relaxed in his chair at a table in Albuquerque's Old Town and talked about how the pandemic changed his life.

The pandemic struck several cops, and a cousin died of the virus. His beat included Old Town, so he also saw livelihoods crash. It made him think of what and who is important in life.

"You see a number of stores who have ... closed," he said. "You kinda think about life differently. Or making plans to go see your family. I haven't seen my mom in a year and a half now.

His thoughts were with his cousin, co-workers, business owners, and his family. It added stress to an already stressful job, but he counted himself as one of the lucky ones.

"If you want to compare my job to others, I think I'm fortunate because I get to go to work every day," he said. "The need for police officers is there. Obviously, over the last year, you've seen a lot of calls for police reform. Some anti-police sentiment.

"And while I certainly understand and appreciate everyone's concerns, I still feel fortunate that I have a job to go to. Because I know that a lot of people just don't have the same opportunities, they lost their jobs. A number of industries have shut down or are greatly diminished."

When he thought of his burdens, he tended to believe others had it worse.

"It's sad because I'd like to see my mom, and I'd like to see my other family members," he said. "But I also know that I'm in a position that I get to continue to work. And get out and see people. I think a lot of people were cooped up and kept inside. As a police officer, I didn't really have that opportunity. I'm thankful I got to stay out and try to help others."

The quarantining and isolation that others felt, he did not experience.

"When I hear about people's stories about having to stay in or constantly being on the computer, ya' know, that's their interaction. I have empathy for them, but I haven't experienced that," he said. "(Those) kinds of changes haven't happened in my life."

But when he thought of the last year, he was grateful that "I'm healthy. I know a lot of people who aren't healthy."

I asked if there were any positives during the year and he took a long pause before answering.

"I don't know of a lot of positives, no," he said. "I'm happy to be here. I'm happy for the friends and family that I have. Certainly, I look at life differently, and I'm grateful for the opportunities that I have ... but not a lot of positives."

It changed the way he policed because he was asked to enforce pandemic restrictions.

"It's one thing for a police officer to enforce laws, but I think to just encourage people is always a lot better," he said. "You get a lot more out of it. I could just walk around and tell everyone to put their mask on right away. Or when it was the height of this, I think just to ask (was best).

"People were already so frantic and kinda worked up about this," he said. "And I think some people forgot ... Just to have empathy and compassion for people goes a long way. Because you don't know what someone else is going through at that moment."

He thought the government's response was mixed.

"I wish we had had a better response," he said. "I think the State of New Mexico has been doing a phenomenal job. I think we're leading the country per capita with the number of people we have vaccinated thus far. So I'm happy with that. I'm happy with the governor's response so far."

As for the future, he relied on Dr. Fauci's recommendations.

"I like listening to Dr. Fauci, and I trust what he says," he said. "But I don't know what the new normal is."

He learned from the pandemic.

"It's a learning experience, to say the least," he said. "I don't have anything profound for you, but I hope you enjoy your ride."

"Live everyday like it's your last"

FARA AND DAVID BORN were living out their credo, "You're not guaranteed tomorrow."

They were on vacation through New Mexico and Arizona when I met them at a Love's truck stop just west of Albuquerque.

Their pandemic was marked by caretaking and tragedy, but they believed most people will adapt.

An ICU wound-care nurse by profession, Fara Born started the year caring for Covid patients at her Colorado hospital.

"I was working in a hospital from March until July 2020, where I'd occasionally take care of Covid patients," she said. "Our hospital would set up special wards."

Fara Born and their 29-year-old son left Colorado for Virginia to home care for her 84-year-old father, who had Parkinson's disease. Eventually, all three showed signs of the disease but were not hospitalized or tested.

David Born may have also caught Covid from his caretaking. Two of his two brothers contracted Covid, and he wasn't sure if he caught it from them.

A brother in Tulsa, Oklahoma, "apparently" caught Covid from a birthday party. The other brother died while suffering from Covid, pneumonia, and esophageal cancer. David Born went to Phoenix to be with him in hospice care.

In what must have been a colossal hospice mistake, David Born was not informed of his brother's Covid positive status.

"I had been there for about five days and then probably the next to last day, they suddenly told me he had Covid," David Born said. "This was kind of a shock to me."

David Born was Covid positive upon returning home. He may have been Covid positive on the flight home, spreading it there.

A Verizon Wireless engineer, David Born was spending "all my time" working from home most of the year. Time outside the house was mainly going to the grocery store, walking the dog, and visiting sick family.

"It's been kinda a stressful year with her dad and with my brother dying," David Born said. "If anything has affected how I look on life and everything, it's been those two people, more so than Covid."

Fara Born was in favor of everything the CDC was recommending.

"My attitude was always, take it seriously and be careful," Fara Born said. "But don't be unduly anxious about it. Be careful, and probably you'll be okay. But like I say, that's from a nursing background, where we are frequently exposed to infectious diseases."

Working in an ICU ward and around deaths, Fara Born said she already had a well-developed belief that "every day is precious."

"You live every day like it's your last," she said, "but you act as if you're going to live forever."

More than ever, she said, "don't put things off until retirement, the things you want to do. Do them now."

They did not like how the Trump administration handled the initial phases of the virus, saying the Trump administration did a "pretty lousy job. There's a lot of talent in there he didn't really take advantage of. And a lot of lies."

However, "Operation Warp Speed seemed to be pretty good," he said.

They both expressed hope things were getting better.

"I think we have more confidence in the government now and hope the CDC will get back on track," David Born said.

He predicted we will "permanently" have to mask on airplanes.

We'll get "some sort of vaccination" every year as the virus mutates. And people will be more understanding and considerate in the future.

"If people think they are getting the flu or something, I think they're going to stay home more," he said. "People, if they feel bad (will mask) if they don't want to give it to somebody else. Or they might feel like they don't want to get anything."

Fara Born worried the lack of vaccinations worldwide will make annual vaccinations in America necessary.

In the meantime, *carpe diem*, seize the day.

"Don't put off until tomorrow what you could do today," Fara Born said, "because you're not guaranteed a tomorrow."

The Humblest Bar on Route 66

I RODE 60 miles west out of Albuquerque and saw roads leading into pueblos blocked off with quarantine signs - No Visitors Allowed.

The sun was going down, and I needed to find a place to pitch the tent. Upon entering Cubero, pop. 289, I saw two churches and a few small homes.

Riding up to the first church, I asked church officials if I could pitch my tent out of sight behind the church. I even used the words " be a good Samaritan." They unceremoniously rejected my request.

Nobody answered the doors at the historic adobe-style church across the street either.

Camping on pueblo lands is illegal, so I was growing more desperate to find a place in town.

I was desperate but kept riding until I spotted the humblest bar on Route 66, the Midway bar.

It is a flat, one-story, concrete, desert-brown lump the size of an intermodal container car. A lonely, square Coors sign hung outside. A black-and-white Route 66 shield was painted on the wall facing the road.

No windows. No artwork. Just a hardcore, no-frills saloon in pueblo country.

Upon entering, I used the same good Samaritan pitch that I used at the church.

This time it worked out better than I could have imagined.

The Midway Lounge manager was Antonio Armijo, a veteran of three tours in Iraq and one in Afghanistan. He shook his head at the story of the church turning down a wayward stranger and gave his thumbs-up to camping behind the store.

The onslaught of the disease meant many local Midway customers couldn't leave their pueblos. The store was reduced to selling packaged liquor, beer and cigarettes.

The bar was closed for six months, and the bar section was still closed..

"This isn't my only income," Armijo said. "I'm a military veteran, so I get disability. But the business owner - it was coming close. He did have to dip into savings and stuff like that. So I know it was an adjustment for them. We had six other bartenders that they had to let go because of the pandemic."

Armijo talked about the economic and personal devastation during the lockdown and curfews at the neighboring pueblos, the Laguna Pueblo and the Acoma Pueblo. Both the infection rate and death tolls were high.

"They (Laguna and Acoma pueblos) took a big toll with the pandemic," he said. "They ended up shutting them down. Putting them on lockdown. Putting them on curfew to kinda stop the spread of the pandemic."

Cubero was originally founded by Mexicans and thrived when the Santa Fe Railroad's first transcontinental rail line was laid alongside the town. These days the area sparsely populated, with 74 percent of the population being either Native American or Hispanic in origin.

North of town is the 11,445-foot Mount Taylor in the San Mateo Mountains, an extinct volcano that's considered a sacred mountain to the Navajo.

The original Route 66 brought vehicle traffic to town before traffic was rerouted by I-40. Historic Route 66 is still Cubero's main street but was lightly trafficked the day I rode through. It felt like an oasis town.

During the year, Armijo developed his own tactics to survive the pandemic.

He was Covid-free, vaccinated, and practiced social distancing. Family gatherings were limited to his immediate family.

"Family is the only ones we've been staying close with," he said. "We haven't really talked to anybody outside the immediate family."

Customers at the store were "in and out," and most were not encouraged to linger inside the building.

The pandemic didn't add significantly to his anxiety, he said, but he was "uncomfortable" with mask-wearing "all the time."

He declined to say if he thought local and federal government restrictions were enough or too much.

"Honestly, personally, I think we're going to have to wear these masks for at least another couple of years until everyone has the vaccine," he said. "In terms of the government (and its response to the epidemic), I try to stay out of politics. I don't really like to get involved."

When his interview ended, his girlfriend Sandee Pasquale offered to tell her pandemic story.

Armijo offered me bottled water and free pizza (which I did not take). I was allowed to set up my tent on a discarded rug behind the bar/liquor store and out of sight of Route 66. After all the drama and beauty of the day, I fell dead asleep.

The Cubero churches were lovely structures, but I found my faith in human kindness with the beautiful souls of the Midway.

Acoma Mom Talks Lockdowns & Funerals

THE MIDWAY LOUNGE turned into the pandemic storytelling theater of Cubero when Sandee Pasquale decided her side of the local experience needed telling.

Pasquale was the Midway manager Antonio Armijo's girlfriend. She listened to his interview from the side of the bar, but she was ready to describe a very different world.

A native of Acoma Pueblo, Pasquale was a mother and a wild-land firefighter in the Zuni Mountains.

"In Acoma, we had a curfew that was from 8 p.m. to 5 a.m. in the morning, and you had to have an 'essential letter' if it was after hours," she said. "We had weekend lockdowns. No one in or out unless you are an essential employee. And no one under 16 can leave the reservation."

Several parents were caught, she said, trying to sneak their children out in their car trunks.

"So they started checking everyone's trunk, and some people would comply and some wouldn't," she said, giggling at the idea.

Acoma posted an alarming number of Covid cases in the first year.

"There was a rise in cases for a while," she said. "They were really strict about it. Having visitors. Even your own family, you couldn't go see your own family for a while. Or I think you'd get like a ticket. So it hit pretty hard."

The previous week, the pueblo reported no cases, so it lifted the daytime lockdown and shortened the overnight curfew. Still, tribal leaders warned restrictions will tighten again if the numbers rise again.

"I guess they're going to see how April goes," she said. "And if we have to go back to the lockdown and back to our curfew."

Pasquale was vaccinated and Covid-free, but her extended family wasn't so lucky. Two months previously, her uncle died of the disease, and pandemic restrictions on his traditional funeral services caused frustration.

"For my family, losing a family member, it was really hard because the reservation has restrictions ... even for people who are from Acoma, to come to funeral services," she said. "That was the only thing really stressful about Covid because we really hadn't had any deaths in our family for a while.

"It had to be on the reservation," she said. "We had all his services there, but it was not like any traditional services that we normally would have."

Striking a balance between Acoma traditions and pandemic restrictions was difficult.

"We have our traditional way of doing things, but with Covid, we couldn't do that," she said. "All the family members who lived off the reservation had to get tested. And if they were negative, they were allowed on the reservation just for the day of the services. And his burial was one day.

"And we had ... another day we had to come back for, but we had to wait a full month for that to happen again, so it was just a long and stressful process to deal with."

Being a mother, she worried that her children were not allowed to leave the pueblo to go to school.

"So I have kids, too, and they're not allowed to leave to go to school," she said. "So my stress level with my kids has been pretty high. And with me having to go back to work because I only work six months out of the year, that's the only stress I've been dealing with."

She wasn't unhappy, but she was very worried for her children.

"Our happiness is (she paused to think) ... I'm happy ... but it worries me about their education because I don't think they're getting the full education they need being all virtual. And that stresses me out."

She predicted that masking was staying around for a long time to come.

"I'm hoping it will be all over," she said, "but I still have the feeling we'll all still be wearing masks, and if we see a rise in cases again, I think it's going to go to how it was this past year."

The local reaction to the lockdowns and curfews was mixed.

"Some people don't like it because ... like when we have the weekend lockdowns, they have to rush to the grocery store to get groceries for the weekend," she said. "Some don't mind at all. Some don't even leave their home. I guess it just depends on the person."

It's the Flu, not the Plague

SHAWNA SAGE LIVED in a camper near the isolated gas station by the I-40 exit, and the pandemic didn't make sense to her.

Sage worked the entire first year of the pandemic at the Milagro Phillips 66 gas station between Albuquerque and Santa Rosa, in the semiarid tablelands along Route 66 across New Mexico.

She stood behind a plastic shield during our interview. The shop store sign asked customers to wear masks and limited the number of people in the station to one person per vehicle.

Sage never contracted the disease, and nobody she knew was infected.

"I don't think it's any more dangerous than the flu," she said. "I think it's a virus. I think that it's going to come back every year. I think if you are old and you have other things wrong with you, maybe they should take better precautions. Otherwise, I think people my age or younger don't have a problem with it."

Masks are unhealthy for you, she said. She referred to a "plague" but never clarified which pandemic she meant.

"They did studies, way back when we had the plague, that the masks are unhealthy for you," she said. "When you breathe your own breath, it's not healthy. Not to mention, some people have asthma. Older people can't breathe anyway very well. I think it's harming more people than it's helping."

She doubts she'll vaccinate. She never got flu shots, so why start now?

When I mentioned the current tally of pandemic deaths, she asked if the people died of the vaccine or the virus. When I told her the deaths were due to Covid, she didn't believe it.

"The hospitals and these places are getting money to have Covid deaths," she said, repeating a trope President Trump used on the 2020 campaign trail. "When somebody dies of something else, they mark that Covid, they get extra money. I don't think that's how it's supposed to go. But I think that's how it ended up being."

Quarantining and social distancing weren't realistic to her.

"I don't see it as an issue," she said. "If you have good hygiene. You can socially distance, you don't have to be in someone's face. I don't think it's airborne. I think if you're sick, you should stay home. If you're not, don't.

"I feel like I'm going to take care of me, you take care of you. I think in the beginning, everyone said, yes, we will do this, because we don't know what's happening. We don't know how awful this is. When we realized this is not the plague, I think people just got tired of listening to the government."

Covid will be "just like the flu," she said. "It's going to come back every year. It's going to mutate. But it's a virus."

She predicted Covid will peter out and all will return to normal. As if it never happened, because it never happened.

"I don't think," she said, "it's any worse than the flu we have every year."

The Afterlife and Evolution of Giraffes

JETT COLA WAS on his way to California to become a star.

He came from the small Tulsa suburb of Broken Arrow, founded when the Creek community was forced out of Alabama on The Trail of Tears.

He was a young, ambitious musician I met at a small gas station in rural eastern New Mexico. He wasn't shy about proclaiming his talents.

"I guess you could say I'm the lead singer," he said. "I rap. R&B sing. Play guitar. Kinda dance like Michael Jackson, but you can't see that right now, you gotta pay for that. Awwe."

I asked if the pandemic set back his music career. He mentioned that his substance abuse got out of control.

"A little bit," he said. "I went and visited my family. Went to jail for a little bit. Just a short amount of time. Stopped smoking weed as much as I did. I started getting too high."

His uncle may have had Covid but Cola said he didn't know anyone else who contracted Covid.

"And I got a big old family," he said. "I got 16 cousins on the one side and another 20 on the other side. Eight brothers and sisters (nobody got Covid)."

Then he made a profane reference to being born alone and now living by a religious code.

"I don't really wear (a mask)," he said. "I live the way God wants me to live. He didn't tell me to wear no mask. I'm only wearing clothes because Adam and Eve had them put the leaf on once they bit that apple."

He was firmly against vaccinations, believing his faith and state of mind will protect him.

"It's a setup," he said of vaccines. "It could be anything, man, you never know. First of all, you're putting it in your body. Why would I do that? I believe in God. My faith is, as you believe, it will happen. So if I start to believe I can catch it ... that's something."

He said he has "the blood of Jesus" over him, so "I'm blessed, healthy."

Cola believed he was warding off the virus by believing he was not vulnerable. He knew a guy who didn't believe in the power of positive thinking, and he got sick.

Cola's year was shaping up well. He met a California woman online.

"I'm going to see her right now," he said, "and make her my girlfriend."

As he spoke, she called on his cell phone, and she listened to the last part of the interview.

"I believe in natural selection, you know, the dinosaurs fell off, you know, that's based off a meteor or something crazy, maybe that's the wrong thing," he said. "But like giraffes. They wasn't going to survive having tiny necks, so eventually, they had to go get a big neck to even eat. So the ones who can't handle it, it's not a bad thing. You get to go to the afterlife, man. There's a lot of pain out here. Just be happy you get to go live in the afterlife."

Pandemic View from a Town of 12 People

DANIEL CHAVEZ RAN the Route 66 gas station in Newkirk, population 12. With the exception of ghost towns, it was the smallest town I rode through on the ride.

There was no Newkirk mayor, but he owned the main business in town. Two cockatiels were warbling and chirping at the back of the store. Route 66 paraphernalia, food, and gas were for sale. A US Post Office was attached to the gas station.

I asked why so few people lived in Newkirk.

"Nobody wants to live here, there's not enough action," he said. "There's no action in Newkirk."

From where Chavez sat behind the plexiglass counter, he was skeptical of the pandemic's death toll.

"A lot of the people who died have not died of Covid," he said. "Some of them, they had other complications besides Covid. People are blowing it out of proportion. I don't think it's as bad as it is. But we have to comply with the rules. But I don't think it's as bad. Been around people who have had it, and they say it hasn't been as bad as they are saying."

His business took all the precautions. He put plexiglass up at the front counter because he said the state required it. He and his family were vaccinated and disease free.

"I see a lot of people every day," he said. "I don't know what they've got. So to protect myself and to protect my family, I got the shot."

He'd heard the conspiracy theories about the vaccine being a way of tracking Americans, but he didn't believe them.

"There's a lot of people who don't want to take the vaccine," he said. "They think it's a chip they put on you. They track you down. We're already chipped. When they gave us our Social Security number, that was our chip they put on us. They can track us down anytime they want."

He was unsure of "what caused it" and how it was transmitted.

"People should not live like this," he said. "They are getting paranoid."

He didn't like it when I asked if the isolation of Newkirk affected his point of view. We get the news, he objected. But then again, he doesn't watch it.

"Just because we're out in the sticks (doesn't mean) that we're not familiar with some of the stuff that's going on," he said. "We see the news. I don't like to see the news that much because it just turns me off."

Negative news, he said, breeds fear, and we should take care to enjoy life, even in a pandemic.

"They (news programs) pounce on this stuff day and night," he said. "It's gotten to the point people don't want to hear it anymore. They just want to shut it off and go on with their lives. It's gotten to the point we cannot live with fear. Life is really short, and we have to enjoy it while we can."

He took comfort that the pandemic wasn't worse.

"When you are young, everything bothers you, but when you get up in age, life is short," he said. "So I try to enjoy every day no matter what goes on. I like being happy. Keep going. What the hell, life is short."

"Not for myself so much as for others"

GLEN HALE and his wife were in Gallup on their way to visit national parks around the country.

I met him at one of the cheapest motels in town, the El Capitan.

Although he was unsure if he had contracted Covid, his wife and brothers did. None of them suffered "anything earth-shattering."

It was a year of adjustments. His music group didn't meet all year, and gatherings with friends were curtailed.

At the beginning of the pandemic, his daughter adopted a child in Texas. He and his wife were conflicted about venturing out. They weighed the risks and rewards. Then decided to visit her.

"We social distanced as much as we could," he said. "Of course, we were in a courtroom at that time, and we were told to keep our distance. But it worked out."

The family also got together for Thanksgiving and Christmas.

An Oklahoma native, he was a vocal music teacher and oil field worker before retiring during the pandemic.

He wasn't unhappy, but he experienced anxiety.

"I have been anxious about family and friends," he said, "and wanting them to be healthy."

The government's response, he felt, should have been handled better.

"I believe there were a lot of mistakes made ... making statements about masks not working," he said. "I don't think it was handled well. I watch the news, and with the variations of the virus that have come about, I'm ready to wear a mask as long as I have to when I'm out in public.

"Not for myself so much as for others. I don't know that I'm (not) carrying the virus, although I'm vaccinated and not sick."

Although there have been adjustments, he felt like his retired life was similar to his pre-pandemic life.

""I'm not a real social person anyway," he said. "Most of the time, if I have free time, I want to be with my family."

Hale didn't know what was coming next, but he knew he'd adapt.

"I see things getting better or not and adapting and continuing safety protocols," he said. "I take things as they come along."

"Get back to the rhythm of life"

OUTSIDE THE WALMART store in Gallup, Ray Cleveland was wearing his bandana as a pandemic mask and showed his Pfizer card as "living proof" of his vaccination.

He was from Window Rock, Arizona, the capital of the Navajo Nation, the largest Native American territory in America. The capital has about 3,000 residents, about a quarter of whom live below the poverty line. It is about 28 miles northwest of Gallup.

"I'm not no half-breed," he said. "I'm a full-blooded Navajo. And that's where my dad became a code talker because he was a full-blooded Navajo (too). And that's how we won the war. We won World War II with the code talkers (Navajo-speaking radio men. The Germans couldn't de-code the Navajo language)."

The first year of Covid devastated the Navajo Nation. Native Americans died about twice the rate of White Americans. Yet Cleveland avoided getting it, and so did his family. He knew how serious it was from reading the *Navajo Times* obituaries.

"The last three days, four days," he said, "zero deaths with Covid."

The Navajo Nation had its own protocols, separate from the CDC, NIH and US government. Cleveland said the Navajo Nation warned that Covid was an "epidemic" in English. Some Navajo Nation restrictions were more strict than the national guidelines.

"That's one of the mandates that the Navajo tribe have," he said, "that you keep your social distancing and wear a mask at all times (even outdoors)."

The nation implemented several 57-hour weekend lockdowns, stay-at-home orders, checkpoints and curfews. Outdoor masking restrictions stretched well into 2022.

The restrictions fit in well with Cleveland's lifestyle and his main weekend passion.

"To tell you the truth, it didn't affect my lifestyle because I like to ride my motorcycle during the weekends, which is doing it by yourself," he said. "You're not going to (motorcycle) in a social environment."

During the pandemic, Cleveland said he saw little of his kids living in Mesa, Arizona, but they stayed connected via Zoom and cell phones. He did not think Zoom calls are going to become the "new normal."

"I think the Navajo Nation is coming out of this, I'm pretty sure," Cleveland said. "I'm pretty sure that we'll get back to normalcy by fall."

The pandemic, he said, reminded people of what's important in life.

"Covid to me was like a wake-up call, for people to get back to the rhythm of life, instead of going crazy and socializing and living the wildlife," he said. "Get back to the straight-and-narrow life, which was taught by our grandparents and the Navajo people. Traditional teachings, get back to that."

Distancing is Nothing to the Lonesome Man

EARL SHURLEY INTENDED to get the vaccine just like he got his "flu shots every year."

"I feel fine," he said. "I know other people I've been in close contact with (who had Covid), and I never contracted the virus."

I met Shurley outside the Gallup Walmart. A local resident, he thought the government's response was good enough.

"I think they've done fine, offering the stimulus checks and all," he said. "It took them a while to get the vaccine developed and everything. And now, it is not even under control, basically. Because I've heard of people who have had the shots, but they still contracted the virus."

Just in case, he was staying away from crowds and even, sometimes, family.

"We didn't have Christmas or Thanksgiving, either one," he said.

The pandemic year didn't affect his happiness level because he was a loner.

"I've always been a lonesome person," he said. "I grew up in West Texas, and I was always by myself ... I've always been a single person. Go out and do it by myself."

He didn't develop any "new hobbies" during the pandemic because he had so many already. He was a trapper, hunter, and hiker. Pre-Covid, he walked the Grand Canyon twice.

His strategy during the pandemic was to stay "away from people who are infected, that I know of. So I stayed healthy. I'm 71 years old, and I've never been sick, hardly, a day in my life."

He credited his robust health history to all the vaccines he got during his military service early in life, including a "black plague" shot.

Covid may be around for years, he feared.

"I have no idea when this is going to end," he said, "because they say there're new strains that's developing, so it could go on another two or three years. It's just hard to say."

"The Whole World Forgot About the Natives"

GALEN PINTO PACKED his pandemic world into a six-minute talk.

He spoke of heartbreak, Native American history, family, economic injustice, community togetherness, depression, isolation, empathy, and death. He decried the politics of vaccinations. And he predicted future pandemics are on their way.

"So many people caught it," he said. "We had a very bad epidemic. It really destroyed a lot of people and people's lives. A lot of people died. At one time, our nation had the highest rate per capita of catching Covid."

I met him in the Walmart parking lot in Gallup and promised the interview would be short. I had no idea he'd been waiting for just this kind of opportunity.

He was from Buffalo Springs, in the Navajo Nation. When several people in his family began dying of the disease, access to their funerals was restricted by lockdowns and curfews. And that, he said, means something different to the Navajo than to most Americans.

"That was very heartbreaking, very heartbreaking," he said of funeral restrictions. "We were very depressed. Native Americans are very touch (oriented) people. We really care about one other. We love each other. We love Mother Earth. We care about each other. And it has devasted us."

The pandemic was a full-blown natural disaster, and the Navajos suffered the most due to poverty and a lack of ready healthcare.

"A lot of Navajos on the Navajo reservation don't even have (drinkable, running) water," he said. "And roads. We have a lot of dirt roads we have to travel and mud and snow and whatever. They can't even get to the hospitals. So many caught it. That's why there's so many per capita that caught Covid."

He also blamed negligence by the US federal authorities.

"The whole world forgot about the natives who live in the United States," he said. "They just plowed over us and just left us."

According to Pinto, Navajo Nation President Jonathan Nez should be given credit for making sure the Navajo Nation reached the "highest" per capita rate of vaccinations.

Pinto got his two Pfizer shots, but his heart went out to fellow Navajos who lived in poor conditions.

"Considering our situations," he said, "a lot of people don't have running water. Electricity. And we live way back in the housing area (using) cardboards and this and that. A lot of Navajos live like that."

He was the son of one of the Navajo Nation's most renowned politicians and activists, John Pinto. He was a "code talker" in World War II. And at 94, John Pinto was the longest-serving representative in the New Mexico Senate before passing away in 2019.

His father fought all his life for economic justice, Pinto said, but the pandemic exacerbated those inequalities and killed many people.

"He helped the Navajo people so much," he said. "We go way back ... People just forgot us. They actually just wanted our land. They didn't care about us. And that is what happened to a lot of natives in the whole United States."

During the pandemic, neglect translated into "they didn't even want to be around us. We were isolated."

His personal unhappiness and stress increased during the pandemic.

"Not being able to see your kids, your family," he said. "I mean, we all had to be isolated. ... It made us realize, don't take things for granted."

This pandemic isn't the end of the suffering, he predicted.

"There's going to be another epidemic again, even a war pretty soon," he said. "You just gotta live life as good as you can and be happy. And try to make things happy with the things you have."

Pinto thought President Trump was negligent but praised the development of the vaccine. He praised President Biden for the vaccine rollout.

"Trump didn't do nothing," he said. "He helped with the virus and all. But once (vaccines) were approved, he should have given everybody shots like Biden's doing. I really thank ... Biden for getting shots to people as fast as he did. If he didn't, we'd have over a million dying of the virus."

Since our interview, more than a million people have died during the pandemic.

Pinto's thoughts went out to others.

"I just pray for all the families that lost loved ones," he said. "Just be strong, and you know, be the best you can. I just pray for them all."

Pandemic Fireman Balances Family & Duty

THE GALLUP FIRE department alarm went off, and Jeremy Padilla dashed away from our interview, jumped into the fire engine truck, turned on the flashing lights, and drove solo out of the station.

Born and raised in Gallup, EMT/firefighter Padilla talked about balancing a dangerous job with his family life in a western town ravaged by the pandemic.

He and his family were pandemic-free, but "trying not to take it home to them" was at the top of his mind.

His 16-year-old daughter was allowed to return to high school, but he decided that since many younger kids were not vaccinated, "I found it wise to just keep her home and continue remote learning."

"This area has been greatly affected," he said. "Surrounding areas, being that it's a border town (with Arizona and the Navajo Nation), we've had a lot of influx into town ... which has caused a lot of spread of the disease."

The changes caused stress on the local public health system.

Gallup's population includes people from the Navajo, Zuni, and Hopi tribes, which suffered high death totals from the pandemic. About 43 percent of the city has Indian roots. It's sometimes known as the "Indian Capital of the World" because of its proximity to the heart of Native American territory.

When deaths spiked during the pandemic, Gallup blocked roads into the town of 20,209 people. Curfews were enacted in the city and in surrounding areas. Vehicles were limited to two people, and residents were asked to stay off the streets except for vital needs.

"It's (the) stress of thinking about the possibility of taking it home," he said. "What are you going to do if you get it? How are you going to adjust your living style? A lot of us have responsibilities, as far as taking care of our families at home. It all comes into play. You're trying to support them, but at the same time but you're trying to be safe also. So it's just really stressful. This is just adding to the type of calls that we experience already."

As an EMT, he treated many people suffering extreme symptoms of Covid.

How a person reacts to a pandemic crisis, he said, depends on a person's perspective.

"You endure the hardships and grow from them," he said. "There's different ways to look at things."

He skirted the issue of whether the pandemic could have been handled better by the government or politicians.

"Not everything is right, and not everything is wrong," he said. "It's always best when people come together to figure it out."

He wasn't sure if Covid was the new normal, but he was sure that he'd adjust to whatever came his way.

"I'm hoping that the vaccine will actually ease the effect of the Covid," he said. "It may be the new normal. But just like the fire service, we're constantly adjusting and changing the way we're responding to calls. There's new tactics and techniques that are always coming up in the fire service. And that's the way we have to be.

"We have to be smart, thinking about the situation and evaluating it constantly. So I feel that's the way we have to be with the whole pandemic until it's actually come to an end - which is maybe, very hopefully, right now."

He was "not necessarily less happy" during the year of trials.

"Just roll with it and hit it head-on," he said. "Just kinda learned to do what you need to do. And take care of your responsibilities. And that's the same thing with this. It's going on. The only way to take care of it is to actually hit it head-on and do what you need to do."

At the end of the interview, I put away the camera just as the alarm went off. Padilla ran for the fire truck.

I picked the camera up and stood filming as he drove a red fire engine truck out of sight to another emergency.

Seeing one man driving a fire truck was a stirring sight. It's a life in service of humanity. Rescue in a pandemic never ends. Hold on. Help is coming!

"Today, let us all count ourselves worthy, / let us number ourselves as so many / standing, not sitting, courage-filled and ready / to move onto a firm ground of forward, / to speak our minds every time / our voices need to be heard."
– Alberto Rios, Poet Laureate of Arizona, 2022

"Every time I think I've seen or learned as much as I can about Arizona, it always turns to new questions and revelations: mountains behind mountains."
– Tom Zoellner, Arizona Native, author of *Rim to River*

MOTHER NATURE, MOTHER ROAD

ARIZONA

I watched a giant tumbleweed barreling down on me like a Covid cell manifested in twisted wood and thorns.

The juggernaut pinballed down the road like a Tasmanian devil with a tailwind and a target.

I moved left, and the tumbleweed veered left. I moved right, and it seemed to know my every move. Another existential threat made manifest.

As the tumbleweed missed my head by inches, I thought I heard on the wind - *"momento mori."*

On another lonely patch of Route 66 I spotted wild horses grazing by the roadside, and one black stallion stood in my riding lane.

Spring was in the air. Was this a stallion in heat looking for a fight? Was this a western showdown?

It was a lonely patch of Route 66, hidden by high red sandstone cliffs. There was no traffic. So I rode into the empty oncoming traffic lane in a wide loop around the stallion.

As I passed the black stallion of the pandemic, I thought I heard it again on the wind - *"momento mori."*

I rode on past the Petrified Forest, Painted Desert, and Grand

Canyon. I couldn't stop because I couldn't interview a natural monument about its Covid experience - or could I?

During the long, slow rides through Arizona's insane vistas, I slipped into madness.

"Mr. Canyon."

"Oh please, call me Grand."

"What has your Covid experience been?"

"Never felt better."

"Why is that? It's a pandemic."

"Bad for people, good for me. I was 'closed' for a while. The air was fresher. The rivers were cleaner. Fewer fires. Truck and airplane traffic dried up. Never saw so much as a single bubble gum wrapper floating on the air."

"You're six million years old," I cried. "You've seen the dinosaurs come and go. Won't you miss us if we get wiped out by pandemics?"

"Suffering is in your nature. It's my nature to be indifferent and beautiful."

"One last question," I queried. "Do you speak Latin? What does *momento mori* mean?"

"Remember that you must die."

"Oh no," I said. "Not today, thank you!"

Okay, that interview was made up so I could show off my Viatorian education. But one thing I know is true about nature - if you listen, nature speaks.

A full quarter of Arizona is on Indian reservations, with 27 recognized tribes. Route 66 runs on or near the Navajo (Dine), Hop, and Hualapai lands through much of the state.

The state is overwhelmingly White non-Hispanic, almost 60 percent. About 31 percent are Hispanic or Latino, 5 percent are Native American, and 4 percent are Black. The biggest employment sectors are trade, transportation, utilities and healthcare.

About 25 miles east of Flagstaff, I rode to the Navajo Blue Travel Center, a gas station, curio center, and truck stop. I tried to stealth camp there. However, a courteous but firm Navajo security guard kicked me off the property - it's on Navajo land.

Night had fallen. I rode over the I-40 bridge not knowing if the land on the other side was Navajo Nation land.

I rode out into the star-lit desert to the distinctive barking and howling of nearby coyotes.

I bedded down for the night on top of my sleeping bag, watching the sky's pyrotechnic show.

The Navajo saw hunting and love stories in their starry sky. The Chinese see mansions, and astrologers see our fates. I wrote a book about traveling carnivals, so I willed the stars to become galactic carousels. Perhaps it was a failure of imagination, but the celestial carnival didn't work for me. I knew they were stars.

I spent the night thinking cosmic thoughts about aloneness, awe, and annihilation.

Later in the night, in a half-asleep state, I couldn't tell the direction of the coyote barks and could have sworn they came from above. Into a dream world I went rising, rising. I rose higher, merging with the Navajo sky if only in my dreams.

Old Route 66 is called the Purple Heart Trail through much of Arizona. I rode through Lupton, Sanders, Chambers, Holbrook, Joseph City, Winslow, Two Guns, Twin Arrows, Winona, Flagstaff, Parks, Williams, Ash Fork, Seligman, Kingman, and over the steep, winding Sitgreaves Pass to Oatman in the Black Mountains overlooking California.

One of the most exalted feelings was riding up near 7,000 feet to Flagstaff. Just north of Flagstaff are the San Francisco Peaks. I oversaw the Coconino National Forest, with the largest stand of Ponderosa pines in the world.

Oatman was a boom town/mining town before the mines closed, and miners set their mining donkeys free. An unintended consequence was that the wild donkeys became a tourist attraction in town.

It's now an old-fashioned western ghost town, with a mock western-style shoot-out on the center of old Route 66. Cowboys shoot blanks. Crowds cheer. Donkeys bray.

Nature and history are remembered together along Main Street, just the way we whitewash it.

Covid on a Corner in Winslow Arizona

TOURISTS TOOK pictures of musician statues and murals in Winslow, referencing the 1972 Eagles song "Take It Easy."

A huge black-and-white "Arizona: US 66" shield was painted over the center of the intersection, in front of the "Take It Easy" tourist display.

Directly across the street was bluesman Tommie Dukes, playing on his electric guitar for tips. In 1997, Dukes was inducted into the Arizona Blues Hall of Fame in Phoenix.

I asked him for an interview, but he said, "No."

He was a real bluesman, more comfortable with his music doing the talking. So he sat down in a chair and started strumming his electric guitar to a blues beat. He improvised his way through personal stories from the heart.

"I just wanted to let you know a little about me. A few years ago, I lost my first cousin to this bad stuff that's going around now. Now, she was in a home down in Tucson, Arizona. My cousin Lucille, she caught it. She passed away. All of you out there, you better believe it.

"It was about January 28th, I believe it was. I lost my granddaughter. She was eight years old in Houston, Texas."

(When a tourist came up to put money in his guitar case, he waved him back.)

"You gotta stand back, bro. I don't have my mask on."

(Dukes went back to his story.)

"I have lost a lot of my friends. Seems like every day somebody's going away. Some people believe it, some people don't. Only time they believe it is when they get it. Then it's too late. They got it.

"I lost some of my schoolmates. It's a terrible thing, y'all, when you lose somebody you love. Someone you care about. Someone that you love.

"And once again, my name is Tommy Dukes, and I'm a bluesman. Just to let you all know, in 1997, I was inducted into the Arizona Blues Hall of Fame, down in Phoenix, Arizona. They called me a North Arizona blues legend.

"We got a band, yeah, but we can't play inside because this stuff is so bad. So this is what I do. I just grab my guitar, come down here, and play for the troops. Nobody can beat nothing. Oh yeah, it's just for you. That's my story. Oooh yeah! Thank you."

He looked up at me with a look that said, "End of interview."

He went on to play traditional blues and popular songs.

His talking blues wandered to other types of illnesses, but he was right to put Covid in the overall framework of all deaths in pandemic times.

It was moving the way he talked about his family, friends, and eight-year-old granddaughter. It didn't matter if they died of Covid. They were deeply personal losses in these pandemic times.

Later, I thought about the artistic way he chose to express himself.

> He lost too many friends, loved ones and family too.
> Covid's not the only thing, that can hurt 'n' kill you.
> Tommy sings of hurt and pain, put it to a blues beat.
> If you want to "Take It Easy," take it across the street.

Words from Beyond the Grave

JOHN CLECTNER WAS TRAVELING the length of Route 66 in his RV on his way to Santa Monica Pier.

Having already traveled 1,500 miles, he felt like he could comment on overall compliance with pandemic protocols. States varied widely in their requirements, but he said most people were masking and distancing.

"Pretty much everybody seems to be complying," he said. "There've been a few places where I have noticed people haven't been, but it's not like everybody. It's just a few. So I think the biggest part of people I've seen have been wearing masks or socially distancing."

He was hypervigilant about watching compliance because he was at high risk due to a pre-existing condition.

"As a lung transplant recipient, I have to wear this mask all the time," he said. "So when this came out, I said, well, I'm not the only one wearing a mask anymore. And when it's over with, I'll still continue to wear a mask."

He was in a Winslow shopping center parking lot when I met him. He was from a small crossroads community, Lewis Center, just north of Columbus, Ohio. His next-door neighbors suffered serious Covid bouts, and one of their parents died. However, nobody in his immediate family contracted the virus. He was vaccinated and Covid-free.

Clectner, age 74, cut back on his social interactions during the pandemic.

"I belong to a bicycle group in Westerville, Ohio, and there's a splinter group of us who rides together all the time," he said. "So we've been doing Zoom meetings every other week or so. Normally, we'd be getting together after a big ride and go to lunch. And socialize quite a bit, and that just has not been going on this year."

Even big holidays, he said, like Thanksgiving and Christmas, were scaled back.

"One or two people (gatherings), and I know where they've been at," he said. "I've been real careful."

He missed his pre-pandemic life.

"Personally, I don't think it's done much of anything," he said. "I live alone anyway. I have a few close friends that I do socialize with, and I do messaging and that sort of thing. And like I said, we do the Zoom thing. The biggest thing is, organized bike rides haven't been going on. So I miss that."

His Route 66 trip was the first traveling he'd done in a year.

"I didn't do any traveling last year at all," he said. "I finally convinced the doctors to let me do this trip this year. So it's getting better."

He picked up a pandemic hobby but was struggling with it.

"Because of all the time I'm spending at home, I took up water painting," he said. "I'm really terrible at it. But it gave me something to do."

He was an optimist about our collective viral future.

"I think if we get to herd immunity, I think things will pretty much get back to normal," he said. "We'll probably be able to take a flu shot, and you'll get the booster shot for the Covid type of flu. So that's what I see happening for the future."

The government's response to the pandemic started out poorly, he said, but was improving.

"I hate to bring up the political section of it," he said. "I think our other president didn't do a great job. I think the new one is doing a real good job, as far as response to it. That's just the way it is. I got some friends who, when this all just came about, basically said, 'This is all just a hoax.' And all that kind of stuff.

"I'm (saying), 'Ya know, I don't feel that way. I'll do what I need to do to stay safe.' And if they want to not ... that's their problem, not mine."

Long after our interview, I received an email from Gail Klauck Jacobs saying Clectner was "set free" on Independence Day, July 4th, 2022. His second lung transplant didn't take.

"Thank you for capturing some of John's vitality," she wrote.

She didn't mention his views on the pandemic or his politics. She didn't bring up anything he said.

She was thankful he was seen.

Being seen and listened is important to people, and it's the way to understand them when we want to sway opinions on future pandemics.

Clectner was seen, and his opinions mattered. He got vaccinated and didn't spread the virus. He let people close to him know how he was thinking, and now people he never knew will know too.

The man is on video to influence people in the future. He speaks to us from beyond the grave, just as all the interviewees will someday when we follow him.

Clectner asked that his ashes be placed in a Chock Full o' Nuts coffee can as his urn. He wanted to end on a good laugh.

Momento mori.

"It's extremely, extremely angering to me"

MARTY ZALEVSKY WAS WATCHING her son playing around Heritage Square when I approached her for an interview.

It was as if we had scheduled the Flagstaff meeting. She was primed to talk the pandemic and kids.

She was a mother of two who changed schools for her children just days before because of the school's new "optional" mask protocols.

"Until this week, my children attended a school called Great Hearts (Academy) in Phoenix, Arizona. It's a charter school," she said. "And our governor has decided to take … some very political steps recently. And instead of erring on the side of science or the recommendations of doctors, he's just getting rid of all the Covid protocols we have in place to keep our citizens safe during this community health emergency."

She blamed Arizona Gov. Doug Ducey for allowing individual schools to make up their own masking rules on pandemic precautions.

"Our school decided that they were going to make masks optional for the students," she said. "Well, my students are second graders and fourth graders, and you really can't put that in a child's hands."

She could give her kids masks and send them to school, but there was no guarantee they'd wear them. And it is certain that many of the other kids would not be wearing their masks.

"When they decided that masks were optional," she said, "I decided they are no longer protecting our children."

At first, the charter school was vigilant about sending out notices about "partnering" with parents to keep kids safe. So the decision to make masks optional was a surprise to her.

"As time goes on," she said, "it seems like everyone is kind of getting sick of Covid protocols, and they've kind of decided to go errant and, you know, fly in the face of science and doctors, which was extremely offensive to me ... and my husband."

The Zalevskys received the school email on a Tuesday and immediately switched schools. By the next day, their children were going to the local public school.

The change was jolting for the whole family. She worried they wouldn't have the same rigor and curriculum. More importantly, she worried about the anxiety the transition might cause her son.

"My son suffers from anxiety, so it was an anxiety-inducing situation to him," she said. "Luckily, he went to the new school, and it was a successful transition. ... It's extremely, extremely angering to me."

She called the changes "emotional" for parents like her.

"Our state is ... not doing a good job of it," she said. "It's very emotional for everybody involved."

She argued her points like the lawyer she was and added the emotional intensity of a mother who felt wronged by the system.

"It's more than just a physical ailment," she said, "it's been a psychological ailment and an emotional ailment, and it's affecting every facet of everybody's lives."

She knew the devastating effects of a pandemic first hand. She contracted Covid in January and considered herself a "long-hauler." She was still struggling to regain her sense of smell and taste.

As a lawyer, she was forced to meet remotely with clients for a while. When I interviewed her, she was vaccinated and back to meeting with clients.

She praised the scientific and medical communities for having thwarted the worst-case scenarios.

"I think the CDC has done an okay job," she said. "You know that it's just been political the whole time. They've had to placate certain politicians and powerful people in offices. I just wish we could have deferred to science and medical doctors on this one."

She found pandemic parenting more rewarding.

"The stay-at-home orders have given us more time to be home with our kids and to parent our kids more hands-on," she said. "It's been great in that sense."

She was going to the park more with her son. He scoots. She roller-skates, which she hadn't done in years.

Her predictions for the pandemic were mixed.

"I don't think coronavirus is going away," she said. "I think it's something we're going to have to live with over time," she said. "And my kids will definitely get their education, but I just don't think I'm going to have the stomach to send them back to Great Hearts."

Looking back on the year, she wished the country's politicians had followed the science. She was grateful the pandemic wasn't even more deadly.

"This is life," she said. "This is one of the things. Every generation has its challenges, and this was just one of ours. And I think in the scheme of things, it was a very light challenge. Thank goodness for science and doctors, but we were able to address it.

"You know, a lot of people lost their lives, and that was really sad, and I'm really sorry for them and their families, but it could have been worse, and I'm proud that it wasn't."

"I think everybody in the world will get it"

WHEN OSCAR ORTEGA CONTRACTED COVID, a high fever, weakness, and hunger kept him home for weeks.

A native of Sonora, Mexico, he was "just visiting" Flagstaff when I met him at Heritage Park.

"I already caught Covid from, maybe, last December," he said. "I stayed at my home for two or three weeks recovering. I felt real tired. You know, hungry. I got fever too."

Ortega's entire family contracted the disease. He heard of people who died of the virus but "nobody really close to me."

"I think everybody in the world will get it ... eventually," he said.

He intended to get the vaccine and thought everyone should do the same. But he believed America will never fully reach "herd immunity."

"I think everybody needs to follow the recommendations," he said. "Everybody has got to wear the mask. Wash the hands. I am going to take the vaccine in the next months or the next weeks."

He thought Mexico's response was weak in comparison to the U.S..

"I think in Mexico, it was not enough, the way the government is responding to the situation," he said. "Here in the Unties States, I think that it's enough, but the government is responding really good. And I think everybody is living with the pandemic right now."

"The worst story I heard"

KATHY AND DOUG SELL were sitting on Heritage Square in Flagstaff on their first vacation of the pandemic.

She was a neurologist, and her husband was a retired judge from Kansas City, Missouri.

The pandemic had an impact on them professionally and personally. Neither of them contracted it, but several people in their extended family fell ill. One cousin died.

Kathy Sell treated patients with Covid.

"I think the worst story I heard was a woman who went out with seven friends before Christmas to a bar," she said. "Six out of the eight (who attended) caught it. She didn't know she had it. Took it to her parents. Her dad, who was my patient, who's about 62, ended up in the hospital for three and a half weeks, very sick. And his wife died."

Kathy Sell was treating more long-haul Covid patients as the pandemic went on. They suffered with "terrible brain fog and hearts racing. And they're depressed and anxious and don't know when it's going to end."

The biggest challenge of the pandemic was keeping up with the changing protocols and science.

"It's like drinking out of a fire hose trying to keep up with all the new medical information coming out because it's something new. And we just don't know about it," she said. "As a doctor, you're trying to keep up every day with new information."

The Sells were both vaccinated. During the pandemic, they didn't go out or visit with friends. They Zoomed and talked on the phone. Doug dropped out of the local Rotary. They wore masks and were socially distancing. They didn't go to church in person.

"That (going to church in person) is coming back next weekend," she said. "I think as more people get vaccinated, those things will come back. And we're here on vacation. So we decided to come out. At least eat outdoors and stay in a motel room. So it's starting to come back."

Asked about anxiety, Kathy Sell jumped right in to share hers.

"I had a lot of anxiety at the beginning," she said. "I was afraid I was going to bring it home from the hospital to my husband. Now that I'm vaccinated, I'm less anxious, but I think it was a year of anxiety. I didn't get depressed, but I got anxious."

Being retired, Doug Sell had fewer high-risk interactions. He didn't "relate to the anxiety."

By contrast, Doug Sell said he was distancing and anxiety free.

"Myself," he said, "I don't relate to the anxiety. I never felt anxious particularly about it. And that might be because, as a retired person, I was home all the time. I hardly saw anybody. Yeah, the depression, it was easy to just go 'Oh, what's the use' and then go to bed ... I feel like things are changing for the better."

Overall, Doug Sell felt healthier.

"I know that, this year, I haven't had a cold. I used to have colds multiple times a year," Doug said. "I think that wearing masks has been a real boon to my health. I think it will be for everybody."

As a couple, their gardening improved. They rehabbed part of their house. They were seeing more of their daughter after she graduated from college and moved next door.

The judge thought the vaccines will become normal, just like the measles, polio, and flu vaccines.

"Nobody ever says a word about (the other vaccines), it's considered normal," he said. "In order to send your kids to school, you have to get them vaccinated against all of it. I don't understand why people don't want to get the vaccine."

When it came to anti-vaxxers, Kathy Sells admitted she was surprised by the number of people not willing to vaccinate.

"I'd say about 20 percent of the patients that I see say they are not going to get it," she said. "Some of them are scared, and they're waiting to see what happens. Some of them are just deniers, and they don't think it's necessary."

Businesses will eventually fully open, Kathy Sells said, and many people will continue masking even when the worst is past.

"I think we're going to get vaccinated up enough that our businesses can all re-open," Kathy Sell said. "I also think that a lot of us are going to be wearing masks when we are indoors, close to other people. I don't know when I'm going to be able to go into a concert again."

"I'm Happier"

DON CONNOLLY WAS SELLING sterling silver and copper-wrapped pendants on the streets of Flagstaff when I met him.

He traveled widely around the country, and he never met a person who later died in the pandemic.

"This was a very interesting year, as far as Covid is concerned," he said. "I've lost about five different people this year. It's really interesting because a lot of people have lost quite a few this year due to a lot of different things. None of which had to do with Covid.

"Which to me, personally, I think it's kind of weird to be in a period where there's a pandemic. Aand we're losing people. Yet I've really only seen a few personal cases of this pandemic taking people out. Which causes a lot of questions for me."

He heard news reports about the virus but hadn't seen the reality of the pandemic. So that made him skeptical of the whole pandemic.

"Yes, we have this thing called Covid," he said, "it's making people sick, possibly killing people, but is it really what we've been told? Is there really a pandemic? Are these vaccines going to be necessary? What is all this actually going on? Why have they shut down all our small businesses and kept all our huge businesses open? It's like, what's the real thing going on here?"

He believed that by living in a school bus, "off the grid," he was better able to see more of the country than most people.

"As somebody on the road and traveling," he said, "I really don't see the cause for concern. I don't see the cause for what is a pandemic."

If he couldn't see the devastation, "I don't see the cause for concern."

He masked up and socially distanced at the beginning.

"I mostly live off the grid and travel and live in the woods, so I do my own part in social distancing," he said. "But really, I mean, I hang out on the streets, and I sell things. And I go to parties. And I hang out and go to places where people are vending ... I've kind of gone on with my life the way it was before."

He thought masking and distancing will go on for a while longer.

"I think everybody is afraid, so, yes (people will mask)," he said. "Because we live in an era where as long as they put it in the media and tell you to do it, then you will. Unless you have a mind of your own. So, yes, I think they will, as long as they are told it's a concern."

He did not intend to get vaccinated. His views were touched with fatalism.

"To me, it's like vaccinating myself for the common cold," he said. "It's just not necessary. I'm young. I'm of good health.

"I also believe that, when you live on this planet, and you live, and you die. You take the time you were put here with to enjoy, and you're taken at the time that you're supposed to be taken. (Be it the) virus, being hit by a car or a plane dropping out of the sky. It doesn't matter. You're here for the amount of time that you're here. That's it."

The pandemic took "my career away from me," he said.

In the pre-pandemic days, he set up concerts, but then the pandemic closed concert venues. He then did what he always wanted to do, buy a bus and hit the road.

"So I've had to lean into my art, instead of making my paycheck that I made every season and contributing as a working part of society," he said. "That has changed extensively in my life. I had to think on my toes and figure out how not to drown because people lost their jobs and don't seem to be getting them back. But other than that, did (Covid) affect my daily living? No."

He insisted that losing his job and wandering the country did not cause him excess stress.

"I'm actually happier," he said proudly. "I'm happier living in between society."

YouTube Censorship of a Far-Out World

ANGEL SANTOS WAS in Heritage Park with his girlfriend and son on a sunny Flagstaff afternoon.

He said no media outlet was covering the truth about the pandemic, but he knew things people never heard of or imagined.

His plethora of conspiracies was too much for YouTube. As a result, they deleted him from *The Story Cycle* channel twice. Regardless, his views are archived on the University of Florida SPOHP site.

To Santos, censorship of his opinions was further proof that he was right.

In his mind, censorship supercharged his beliefs and turned him into the holder of truths not available to the rest of the world.

"It (Covid) was orchestrated long ago, and right now they are terraforming the planet with chemtrails (indecipherable) and now inside us with the vaccine for an agenda beyond what we can see in the mainstream media because it is controlled by major corporations."

The hidden realities behind the cons, manipulations, and appearances of this world were real, but Covid was not real. Nor were the benefits of distancing, masking, and vaccinations. I asked if he took any of those measures.

"No, definitely not," he said.

Sitting in Flagstaff's central public area, he said healthy living and belief in God were his protection against Covid.

"That's why I'm out here getting this vitamin D (from the sunshine)," he said, about sitting outside in the park. "Keeping my immune system (strong) and eating plant based. Doing what God gave us, not what man gave us."

The pandemic death toll was being faked as part of a worldwide conspiracy, he said. The pandemic wasn't happening. There were no additional deaths.

He seemed to be claiming that Bill Gates, Big Pharma, Monsanto, Big Tech billionaires and the WTO were orchestrating the pandemic hoax. However, even they were manipulated by others behind them, still another shadowy cabal.

Knowing all this, I asked, where do we go from here?

"Operate with love," he said. "And most importantly, treat one another with love, because, one thing that's happening is they're dividing everybody up. Making everybody hate each other. It is easier to control people, dividing us all up. So the first thing is, getting back to loving each other and not hating each other."

(Santos's views were censored by YouTube and can be found on the SPOHP website)

"This was a devastating year"

ISRAELI-AMERICAN SAM FRISHER lived in America for 42 years but never saw hard times like these pandemic times.

He owned the El Trovatore in Kingman, which has a 206-foot Route 66 map painted along the length of the motel. It's one of the most popular roadside attractions on Route 66, but Covid nearly sent the historic motel into the history books.

Frisher and his wife were so in need of funds that he was "using my wife's social security" to keep up their mortgage loan payments.

"In the last nearly year and a half, we had almost no travelers," he said. "We used to get people from all over the world."

The motel features 50 ranch-style units in one story. Before the pandemic, the motel was completely full for an average of ten months a year.

During the pandemic, El Trovatore rented out half its kitchenette rooms to locals who were housing unstable. Arizona had pandemic-era restrictions on evicting people who didn't pay their monthly motel bills. The motel had boarders but, sometimes, no money coming in.

He did not apply for a PPE loan, a Small Business Administration loan program for small businesses during the pandemic.

"We just stayed in our room and survived it somehow," he said.

He spoke from behind a plexiglass window, and he masked all day. He and his wife were in their 60s and fully vaccinated and Covid-free. Yet Frisher, a diabetic, felt particularly vulnerable because he was dealing with the public all day.

He admitted to suffering from anxiety during the year.

"Of course," he said, "this is a normal thing that you don't sleep nights, and you think that you are not breathing or whatever. And that is part of, basically, anxiety because of this Covid news."

He blamed some of the pandemic problems on the numerous sources for Covid news. Some news, he said, was conflicting.

"Basically, the United States has the mistake of having too much information from everywhere, like the internet," he said.

The pandemic, he said, carried some hard lessons.

"You learn to appreciate the person next to you more than what you were used to," he said.

Frisher was derisive of President Trump floating the idea of injecting "bleach" into your veins. He called on people to come together to fight the pandemic, "because we live on the same planet."

His motel business will not fail, he said, because America is coming back stronger than ever.

"We'll survive it," he said. "The motel business will continue. Arizona will recover because in Arizona we have ... the Grand Canyon, and places like a Sedona."

Honey Sweetens the Conspiracy Pot

IN A TINY, remote honey shack in the Mojave Desert sat Harold P. Boushell, who claimed to be the most independent thinker you'll probably ever meet.

"I'm the richest homeless person you're going to meet," he said. "I live in a Blue Bird bus. I'm completely isolated from humanity. I'm not isolated from the internet. I threw out my TV set in 1994. A black and white. Antennae coat hanger. Just dropped it in an incinerator. I've been thinking independently since 1994."

He was an anti-vaxxer because of "mRNA" technology, the manipulation of ribonucleic acid molecules, a basic element of life.

"All those vaccines are experimental," he said. "They are beyond experimental. They have no idea of what they are talking about."

Boushell wasn't the run-of-the-mill honey shop clerk. Before living off the grid in a school bus, he was a computer engineer in the 1960s.

His mind was cleared of the noise of the world, he claimed. His isolation in the desert and computer expertise gave him his clear-eyed vision.

"I'm not confident they (vaccines) work, and they are dangerous," he said. "It's been proven ... a baseball player has died, and some kind of recent guy has died."

He was skeptical about the death toll from the pandemic and

believed that Microsoft billionaire Bill Gates was "suspiciously compromised by the New World Order."

"Covid is real, but the numbers and the propaganda is fake," he said.

He believed vaccines hurt pregnant women, kill healthy people, and end up with a "new world order."

"We're going to have a problem," he said, "indefinitely."

"Going forward, a lot of women are going to be sterilized," he said. "And a lot of people are going to die due to the second shot ... They (the government) are just doing a power grab. Actually, it's the world government."

There will be a civil war, he said, touched off by the world government overreaching and people rising up to resist it. He predicted violent times soon, not "25 years" into the future.

If and when his apocalyptic vision comes true, he said, nobody will be able to find him in his Blue Bird school bus hidden out in the Mojave Desert.

"Just don't trust Biden," he said, "and question everything the government does."

(Author's note: Boushell's views were deleted from the YouTube channel but can be seen on the SPOHP website.)

Guns, Rocks and Art of a Desert Enigma

JACK NORTON RAN a polished rock shop on a table next to the Cool Springs souvenir shop at the foot of Sitgreaves Pass.

As the owner of Raw Rock Creations, he wore a cowboy hat, a six-shooter in his holster, and another handgun in his pocket.

Norton distrusted most outside sources of information.

"All I got to go by is what they tell me on the TV," he said. "I don't believe what I hear on the news, so it's hard to understand what's going on in other parts of the world. I live out in the middle of nowhere. I live out in the mountains."

In town, he lived by "their" rules. But out in the Mojave, he lived by his.

"I find it as being another one of them flus they just ain't got the right vaccine for," he said.

He was frustrated that he couldn't trust the federal government or the media.

"All them people that lost family members, I'm sorry, but you know, I think our government has a lot to do with this. They ain't telling us all. The news ain't telling us all. And we have to play this hit-and-miss, what's-going-on game."

He thought the federal government "wants control of us" and "our money." He carried two guns and had more at home so he could defend himself against burglars and government overreach.

"I do not use a bank," he said. "I don't use a lock and key, I use guns and dogs."

He was a confirmed anti-vaxxer.

"Ain't no way you're sticking one of those needles in my arm," he said. "Jesus, folks, think about it, you don't even know what they're putting into these masks that they tell you to put around your face."

As for the vaccines, "how do you know they don't have a microscopic chip tracking device in there?"

He saw no reason to get the vaccine because he was healthy. He talked to "Mother Nature" about it, and he believes "there will be repercussions," but he didn't elaborate.

Norton was suspicious of other flus, too, including the bird flu and swine flu. He said they appeared during election seasons.

He added that he was suspicious of the "numbers" during the last presidential election, in which former President Trump falsely claimed the election was stolen.

He feels for all the suffering out there.

"People are losing their homes," he said. "They have nothing. They've lost a year. Think about 14 months. No job. No money. All they've been doing is pay, pay, pay, pay, pay. I myself, I see this as a government fucking takeover. It may take a long time, but the ball is rolling. Look at the big picture, it's obvious."

He was positive that the federal government was withholding the real pandemic cure.

"They have an ultimate vaccine somewhere" but "won't share that because that means they've lost their control."

With all the fear of outsiders, the government, and the media, I was shocked when he picked out a bloodstone for me. He wrapped the bloodstone in string and wire. Then he placed it around my neck.

"What do I owe you?" I said.

"Nothing. Good luck."

The poet Natalie Diaz wrote in one of her poems that the Navajo believe bloodstones cure snakebites and stop bleeding.

I hung the bloodstone cure around my neck and rode off with my Navajo mojo. I'm wearing it now as I write, because you never know when the serpent might bite.

(*YouTube canceled Norton's video interview on The Story Cycle channel. His full interview is on the SPOHP archives website.*)

A Desert "Hippy" Calls for Covid Peace

His name was Gerald W. Evans Jr., but his friends call him the "G-man."

He was hanging around the rock shops and curio shop at Cool Springs. Once a filling station, it's a Route 66 landmark.

G-man had just "one opinion" on the pandemic.

"It's just about the mask thing," he said. "Everyone can wear a mask, and I'm fine with that, but don't force me to wear one - like I don't get that at all. If you got your mask on, you're protected, right? You know, so why do I have to wear one?"

He didn't mask and won't vaccinate.

"I never get vaccinated for the flu or anything like that," he said. "I don't trust putting anything into my body. I'm kind of a hippy."

When he looked back on the pandemic, he saw a significant fallout.

"Everybody is losing jobs. People are losing homes. I've managed to stay and work but, you know, lucky me," he said, adding that he worked as a tree climber.

I asked about the government's response to the pandemic, and Evans responded with a story about the McDonald's restaurant in the Prescott Valley area.

"They were fucking super dicks about not wearing a mask," he said. "I just wanted to get a burger and eat something."

He found it difficult to understand the scope of the pandemic death toll.

"I look at statistics, and it might be fucked-up for me to say, but how many people die in car crashes every year?"

It's more important, he said, to enjoy ourselves now.

"The only thing certain in life is death," he said. "So we gotta enjoy our world while we can. Try to treat everyone with kindness."

He enjoyed a good "conspiracy" theory.

"I haven't figured one out yet. When I do," he said, "I'll let you know."

He signed off from the interview with a shoutout celebrating April 20th, an informal marijuana celebration date.

"Happy 420! Happy 420! Yeah!"

Existential Questions & Donkeys

SOMETIMES IT SOUNDED like the donkeys were mocking us when they brayed in Oatman. They stood next to Jamie Slocum and me as we spoke about the death toll from the pandemic.

Hee haaaw!

Underlying health conditions. Vaccines. Politics. The Meaning of life.

Hee haaaw!

Slocum was an anti-vaxxer and anti-masker from Minnesota. He was in Oatman for the day, he laughed, "looking at the donkeys."

Oatman is a former gold mining boom town abandoned long ago, but the donkeys that worked the mines were left to fend for themselves in the Black Mountains.

Now the donkeys are part of the old Western town tourist trap. There are 131 ghost towns in Arizona. The people come and go, but the donkeys stay.

Slocum believed vaccinating was less of a health risk to him than to older people who "should take care of themselves."

He was not wearing a mask for the interview, so I asked if he ever wears masks.

"In Minnesota, we have to wear a mask because it's the mandate," he said. "I'm glad we're in Arizona, where it's not mandated. That's about the only change. In general, things haven't changed. We still go to work."

He was not vaccinated because he didn't believe it was safe.

"I still think the government may be testing," he said. "And I'm not prepared to be tested on. I think 20 years from now, there's going to be an ad on TV where the attorney is asking, 'If you were part of the first round of vaccinations, we can help you get money from the government.' So I'm not willing to get into that."

Different masking and vaccine policies from state to state made Slocum question the efficacy of pandemic measures.

"I personally think that if you're older, you should take care of yourself," he said. "And the government should not take care of everybody. North Dakota had a mask mandate, and South Dakota had no mask mandate. And (South Dakota) stayed open for business. North Dakota did not. And you really can't tell a huge difference in the numbers of cases.

"I read about the older people," he said. "What was the number, 78.6 (years old) was the average age of dying from Covid, and that's the average age of people dying in the United States. Kinda weird how it's the same."

He socially distanced at the beginning of the pandemic but was not anymore.

"The government put us in a big lockdown," he said. "Like, whoa, you gotta do this. So we did it for the first three weeks, or whatever it was, in Minnesota. After that, we just kinda did our thing."

I brought up the latest death toll numbers and asked if they made him more aware of his own mortality.

"No," he said. "I feel bad for people who died, but most of them had underlying conditions. And I don't know how you fix that. Masking people up and shutting down businesses so people lose their way of making money, and all that, I don't know if that's the right way either."

I asked if he'd ever vaccinate.

Hee haaaw!

"Not till we know more about it," he said. "Look at the (Johnson & Johnson vaccine), the single-shot one, and all of a sudden, everyone is dying of blood clots. Apparently, they didn't get everything figured out before that happened."

(*Slocum was referring to the temporary pause in the use of the Johnson & Johnson vaccine after the blood clot deaths of six women ages 18 to 34.*)

I asked him when he thought things will return to normal, if ever.

"Nobody knows," he said. "That depends on the government. What they tell us we can and cannot do. I'm not really a government follower. Or a rule follower. But when the store tells you have to do it, you have to do it if you want to go to their store."

He thought the restrictions should have been lifted long ago.

"We're already in the end stages (of Covid)," he said. "It's more of an endemic than a pandemic."

I respect all opinions so generously offered. Do not mistake the addition of the braying to this report as a comment on the views of Mr. Norton. I cannot thank him enough. His views are valuable.

Besides, I don't think those asses know what they are talking about.

"When Mojaves say the word for tears, we return to our word for river, as if our river were flowing from our eyes. A great weeping is how you might translate it. Or a river of grief."
— **Natalie Diaz, a native of Needles, from her book Postcolonial Love Song, winner of the 2021 Pulitzer Prize.**

"We were somewhere around Barstow, on the edge of the desert when the drugs began to take hold."
— **Hunter S. Thompson, Fear and Loathing in Las Vegas.**

DESERT BONKS TO MOUNTAIN HIGHS

CALIFORNIA

*M*isjudgment in a time of pandemic can be fatal. So, too, when crossing deserts.

Riding out of the Black Mountains on the border of Arizona, I passed through the Navajo Valley across the Colorado River through Needles, Goffs, Fenner, Amboy, Ludlow, Newberry Springs, Daggett, Nebo Center, Barstow, and Victorville.

Not far outside of Needles, I "bonked" in the Mojave Desert. The term bonked is bicycling slang for not being able to ride any further. Between Needles and Goffs, I stopped to rest several times on sandy roadside embankments.

When I finally made it to the Goffs Cultural Center, it was closed and gated. No water. No shade.

I laid down in the desert sand on the roadside with my red bandana over my face. It was 100 degrees. The sun was sucking the life out of me. I was in danger of heat exhaustion.

Then, as if driving out of a mirage, an older man in a golf cart stopped by my side.

"My wife and I," he said, "are caretakers over there (at the cultural center). Come on. We'll give you water and a sandwich."

Not only did I regain my strength, but Morris and Judy Swain raised my spirits too. They went back to their home to get their guitars and returned with a show for me. They sang a gospel song and "Route 66."

They saw I was feeling better, so they challenged me to tell stories and songs. I may have told more stories and sang more songs than they did. The day went from near disaster to one of the best days of my life.

There was even a tailwind when I got back on the bike. I rode like a new man to Najah's Desert Oasis, a truck stop near the ghost town of Fenner. I camped the night in a grove of desert palm trees.

On day two, I bonked again near an I-40 underpass. I stopped to lie down in the shade of the bridge. A passing stranger stopped to give me an orange and some water, which raised me like Lazarus from the dead.

I rode to the next ghost town of Amboy. There are 346 ghost towns in California, and by then, I feared becoming a permanent resident of one.

On day three, I rode and walked to the next ghost town, Ludlow. There's a motel, café, and Chevron gas station at the I-40 turnoff.

I rebounded by morning but rode the rest of the next day like a prize fighter who knew what it was like to be knocked out - three times.

Victorville is the end of the High Desert and the beginning of the ride up to the Cajon Pass, between the San Gabriel and San Bernadino mountains. The view of the mountains from the pass is spectacular, and on the far side is Greater Los Angeles.

For the first time, I looked back on the road and all I experienced in this leg of it. I'd been mistaken for a dead man several times in the Mojave Desert. I almost dried up like the bleached bones in a Georgia O'Keefe painting.

I rode out of the Mojave in love with deserts.

"Out Here in the Desert"

JUDY SWAIN and her husband Morris lived all their married life within ten miles of the Goffs Cultural Center.

Semi-retired, they were caretakers for the center that hosts events for the Mojave Desert Heritage & Cultural Center and the nearby school house museum.

Judy Swain knew more than a dozen people who contracted Covid. Her niece and a good friend were hospitalized.

She and Morris masked and distanced during the pandemic. She believed they were Covid-free unless they were asymptomatic during the year and didn't know it.

When Judy Swain talked about her opinions and her life, she included her husband in the answer. So she'd say, "we" are skeptical of the vaccine.

"We're not sure that it's foolproof yet, safe," she said.

They were waiting until "we feel right about it."

"I think it wasn't tested long enough," she said. "And out here in the desert, we're just a little bit skeptical. Probably a lack of trust ... we are still undecided."

Short of vaccinating, she and Morris were isolated by their desert lifestyle. Still, they masked up when near the public.

"I think we tried to take precautions," she said. "And if you follow the precautions, you're pretty much safe. We are very isolated out here. We don't go to town very often."

The isolation called for by the pandemic restrictions fit the couple's lifestyle.

"We're kinda loners, so it doesn't bother Morris and I too much," she said. "We like our solitude."

All she can do, she said, is hope for an end to the pandemic.

"We certainly hope that it's going away," she said. "And that's all we can do right now, wait and see."

Off-camera, she added that she believed her faith in God helped them through the pandemic.

Dodging Covid & Tracking Desert Bighorns

As HE DROVE through the Mojave Desert in his white pickup truck, Rick Ianniello was on the lookout for desert bighorn sheep suffering from their own version of a deadly virus.

To his surprise, he spotted an even rarer site - a bicycle rider, dressed entirely in black, was lying in the shadows of an I-40 overpass.

Ianniello offered me an orange, a water bottle, and encouragement. The desert ghost town of Amboy was just a few miles ahead.

Amboy is a Route 66 landmark with a working gas station where I could restock on snacks and water. It was slightly downhill, and there was a slight tailwind.

Ianniello was following the local population of desert bighorn sheep, many of whom were suffering from mycoplasma ovis. He called it a "respiratory illness, that comes from domestic sheep but is pretty prevalent throughout the desert, at this point."

At one point, Covid blocked his ovis tracking.

"Last fall, when we were doing some work with the bighorn, I was supposed to be out here for two weeks helping with disease monitoring work for the sheep, not for Covid," he said. "But my roommate's boyfriend got Covid and was over at our house. And I was exposed, so I was quarantining for a couple of weeks. But fortunately, I didn't get it."

The quarantine meant he missed the helicopter roundup of bighorn sheep that season. He made it sound exhilarating, like stuntman work.

"They fly the helicopter up next to the sheep with a net gun," he said, "shoot the net gun out of one side, then they'll spin the helicopter around and jump out of the other side."

Already vaccinated, he found socially distancing was easy most of the time. He was on the lookout for bighorns, avoiding people.

"I've been socially distancing" he said. "Sometimes, it's having get-togethers with friends in their backyard or outside or hikes or something. I haven't seen my parents in a little over a year. They are back in North Carolina, and I haven't been able to travel."

Socially distancing was the norm where he lived in his small, rural California town.

"I don't have much of a problem being by myself," he said. "Living in a town of 10,000 people, it's been pretty easy."

The Mojave Desert, named for the Mojave people, covers 25,000 square miles of land in southeastern California and portions of Arizona, Nevada, and Utah. The desert is one of the oldest places on earth, with landscapes 2.7 billion years old, more than half the age of the earth. During the Paleozoic era, the Mojave Desert was underwater.

I expected the triple-digit heat and desert basin, but I was knocked out by the mountains and buttes, scores of them rising out of desert moonscapes like the panoramic opening scene of an American western movie.

The old Route 66 still exists in the Mojave, weaving its way around and through the mountain passes. Along some portions, construction forced me ride on I-40.

As an environmentalist tracking a mammal virus, Ianniello might be expected to have an insight into Covid, but he was unsure of its future path.

"I personally don't know," he said. "I'm 50-50 on whether the vaccines take care of it and then it fades away, or maybe eventually gets eliminated. Or are different variants of the virus going to cause a problem? Maybe something that's resistant to the vaccine. And having to develop new vaccines during different periods of spikes and lulls of the virus. It seems like it's really hard to say at this point."

With a master's degree in public health, he said he's "in line with the mainstream advice on masking, distancing, and vaccinations."

Ianniello drove ahead of me and set up his high-powered telescope on a tripod.

I rode up to his viewing spot and dismounted.

"Look, you won't believe this," he said.

I peered through the telescope. A desert bighorn sheep stood staring back at me from the Marble Mountains a few miles away.

Like the bronze lions outside the Art Institute of Chicago, the desert bighorn sheep cut a regal stance.

They have keen eyesight. The bighorn froze on the mountainside. It knew it was being scrutinized from the road.

I wondered if the bighorn had Covid. I wondered if it, like me, was suffering in the desert and needed Ianniello's helping hand.

The sight of the desert bighorn sheep inspired me, and I rode resurrected the next few miles to the ghost town of Amboy.

Vaccine Roulette

THE SHANNONS WERE DEALING with Covid the best way they knew how, by doing their own internet research and listening to people they trust.

They decided to follow all the guidelines but one. Their sources told them that vaccines kill perfectly healthy people.

"There are more negative results from (vaccines) than positive," he said. "There are videos on Facebook and YouTube all the time regarding people being completely healthy, getting vaccinations, and the next thing you know, they're sick. And they're in the hospital. And they die."

I met Thomas Shannon in the Barstow Walmart parking lot. He'd driven in from his home 20 miles away in the Mojave Desert, in a town named Hinckley.

He knew vaccines didn't kill everybody, but each shot was like playing a suicide game of chance.

"It's like playing Russian roulette with your life," he said. "Do you really want to put that bullet in the gun, spin it, pull the trigger and find out, when you don't even necessarily have to play Russian roulette? Just don't get the vaccinations."

The Shannons knew firsthand how tragic the pandemic could be. Shannon's wife was a long-hauler with ongoing "breathing, coughing, hacking." His 16-year-old daughter's Covid cough made her sound like a chain smoker.

His wife remained unvaccinated because she believed that having Covid made her immune to future bouts of Covid and its variants.

"She's already had Covid," he said. "There's no reason for her to get Covid if her body has already built up an immunity to it,"

Thomas Shannon caught Covid and experienced "mild" symptoms, which convinced him he had an adolescent's immune system.

"There's no point in getting a vaccination for something I already (had)," he said. "All of my doctors have told me that I have a high immune system ... Basically, my organs and my kidneys are as good as an adolescent. And I'm 39, almost 40. I've never gotten any other vaccinations ... and I've never gotten sick."

Except for Covid that one time.

Masking and distancing were essential to Shannon, so he and his wife missed visiting their family and friends during the holidays.

His parents and daughter were not vaccinated. It hurt him that he couldn't go and help them.

"My mom and dad are in Ohio," he said. "And they are trying to force the vaccinations of the people out there. And my mom, my dad are like, 'No!' ... it's not good."

Perhaps paradoxically, some aspects of their lives have gotten healthier. His wife lost 160 to 200 pounds, and her snoring and sleep apnea disappeared. His "rotten" teeth were pulled.

"Just in general," he said, "this year we're getting our health a lot more improved."

He believed Covid aggravated racial tensions that didn't exist when he was young. Instead of uniting the country during a crisis, the pandemic was dividing it.

"People need to take the sticks out of their butts and come together more as a nation," he said. "Life goes on. Life goes on."

"I got God on my side"

ANDREW SEGA WAS CORRALLING shopping carts when I asked him if he wanted to talk about the pandemic.

He was suspicious at first.

I worked harder for his interview than any on the trip. Does someone else's opinion mean more than yours, I asked? Don't your ideas matter? Let people hear your voice. Be seen.

Sega came back two hours later on his ten-minute rest break, still wearing his blue medical mask outside. Sega, 18, originally from Riverside, California came back and spoke his mind.

"I had Covid before. And the symptoms that I had were not having taste. And I wasn't able to smell," he said. "So Covid is serious. It's real," he said. "It didn't hurt. You can't taste or smell. It's not painful ... Those are the symptoms I've had."

He and his friends had gotten sick, and a relative died of Covid.

All this convinced him to mask and distance, but he was vaccine hesitant.

"I feel like since I already had it, you know, I might be able to get it again," he said. "But I got God on my side. I'm good."

He believed in masking, distancing, good nutrition and God.

"God is with me," he said. "And also, it's about taking care of yourself. Staying six feet apart, away from people. Having your mask on. Being safe. You know, following the rules. You know, do what you're supposed to be doing."

Sega worried about the side effects of the vaccine. He believed he had more to fear from the vaccine than another bout with Covid.

"I don't know how it really works," he said. "I have to do some, what do you call it, researching. It might have some effects on me. I don't want to risk that."

I asked if he was aware that many African Americans chose not to get vaccinated, but he said he had not heard that. He said the pandemic was rough on his personal life.

"It's been a kind of hard, you know, but family is very important," he said. "So I stay with my family. But it's been a little hard. I won't lie."

I asked if he was less happy this year or last year.

"I'm the same, sir, still the same."

Did the pandemic change him in any way?

"No. Like I say, I'm still the same," he said. "Just staying positive. Still the same. This Covid has no effects on me, you feel me. I'm still strong."

Did any good come from the pandemic?

"Any good?" he seemed surprised. "I mean, I got a job. That's a good thing. I got a job. So that's basically it. I'm still here, breathing."

He had no strong opinions on whether the federal and state governments were overreaching or not on Covid.

"They're doing what they're doing, that's it," he said. "Everybody knows about Covid. So they're doing what they're doing."

As for the future, he took a laid-back approach.

"I can't predict the future," he said. "Whatever happens, it happens. Just stay positive."

He believed the pandemic was hurting his generation. Too many people are isolated inside, playing video games, and not getting out. Socialization was lacking.

"This Covid, it affects everybody in the house," he said. "Some people are scared. There is a lot of kids. They inside playing video games. Not being active. And not being able to get to school, not being able to communicate with other kids. Everybody communicates on this technology. I don't know if that is really healthy for us, to be honest."

Covid is complicated, he said.

"You know, some people need to learn how to socialize and communicate," he said. "And communication is really important, but it's just a lot of things. Everybody has got to get acting. It's just a lot, man. That's basically it."

Carnival boss says, "Make sure you live!"

MARK LUNDGREN WAS the general manager of a traveling carnival setting up in a parking lot on the eastern edge of Barstow.

A native of Santa Monica, he took a seat on the steps of a trailer while his carnival was setting up for a Cinco de Mayo festival.

California adopted some of the most restrictive pandemic rules for traveling carnivals in the country. Paul Maurer Shows closed in March 2020. Barstow was its first post-shutdown show.

"We didn't do a show, but we worked on all of our equipment, updating, upgrading everywhere we can," he said, working without a full salary for the year.

Pandemic restrictions mandated additional sanitizing (cleaning of ride seats), capacity limits and food restrictions.

"This county is not giving out temporary food permits," he said, due to pandemic rules.

The carnival was expected to be fully staffed by the end of the week, both with Americans and H2B visa workers en route from Mexico.

He was looking forward to a big comeback during the summer.

"I think we'll do alright," he said. "Most people are over the lockdown phase of this coronavirus, and I think we're going to have a really good summer. I'm very optimistic."

A 20-year-veteran of the carnival business, Lundgren said he was not vaccinated.

"A, I've already had the Coronavirus, and, B, I was blessed with an immune system," he said.

Covid rampaged through his family. His wife, both sons, both daughters-in-law, and grandkids contracted the disease. He credited his "very good immune system" for his Covid symptoms being mild.

Lundgren predicted there'll be vaccine side effects in the future, and he was more afraid of the vaccine than another bout with the disease.

"They call it a vaccination," he said. "It's an experiment. It's approved for experimental use. For emergency use. It's just not a vaccine. A vaccine goes through years of trials. Years of testing. Not (just) a year. Politics aside, Republican. Democrat. It doesn't matter. You can speed up a process so much, but at the end of the day, we don't know. Ten years from now, you're going to watch the news, and you're going to hear, 'If you took the Covid vaccine 2019, 2020, 2021, you might be entitled to compensation.' And that's not going to be me."

He didn't socially distance or mask during the year either. He hung around with like-minded people.

"If the liberal logic were true," he said, "we'd all already be dead anyway."

There has been some good to come for the year, saying he "takes the good out of everything."

"We've been off for a year and a half," he said. "I've seen my grandkids every day for that year and a half. I've been to my boat every weekend during that time. I just take the blessings as they come."

The government response was subpar, he said.

"Initially appropriate," he said. "After the 'two weeks' to flatten the curve. Everything else has just been hogwash. Political power."

He was cynical about an announcement by the City of Los Angeles that the pandemic numbers had gone down enough to temporarily loosen restrictions.

"It's amazing," he said, "when you're facing a recall (California Gov. Gavin Newsom faced and survived a recall), you start opening up your state."

Asked if his life changed at all that year, he was ready with a quick answer.

"If you look at Florida and Texas, both were left wide open and still have less numbers than California and New York," he said. "And you look at population demographics, everything else, they're pretty equal."

He had words to live by for people wondering how to respond to Covid.

"Don't spend your life building a life; spend your life living your life," he said. "We're all going to die one day. Whether you die of coronavirus, in a car accident, or of natural causes, you are going to die. Don't forget to live."

The entertainer was advocating for life.

"They have that saying, 'You only live once.' I disagree. You only die once. Make sure you live."

Covid Birth, Death and in Between

A NURSE in hazmat gear was her first visitor after Rashonda Martin had her baby. Within 24 hours, they rushed her out of the hospital. It was a Covid-era birthing.

When I caught up with her in Barstow, she was unvaccinated and never wanted to be.

She conceded that the FDA ruled the vaccines safe. She recommended the shot to others. She cited pro and con arguments on vaccinations.

"The same people who approve your groceries, your medicines, all this kind of stuff, is the people that's in charge of making sure this corona vaccine is safe for our people," she said. "I trust what the FDA says. The FDA is who is going to approve this medicine, correct?"

However, she wasn't sick, so why should a healthy person get the vaccination if it might make her sick or kill her?

"I believe in it," she said, "but if I don't have the symptoms and I don't have reasons to take the shot. Like the flu shot. I didn't take the flu shot because I didn't get the flu.

"It seems like everybody who gets vaccinated with something they usually have to go through the (side effects) because the virus is now in your body. So your body's got to go through the red blood cells and the blue blood cells to make sure it's not attacking your body and all that stuff. You know the science and all that stuff."

She did her own research.

"But if you didn't know those types of things, you wouldn't know, like 'Should I get it because the people say so, or shouldn't I get it?' ... From my research, if I get the virus and need a shot, I will take the shot. But if I do not get corona in my system, I do not choose to put the coronavirus in my system. That's just my personal opinion."

She thought other people should get the vaccine and didn't think the government went far enough to make people mask up. She said the government had to learn from the virus as it went along.

She could foresee people masking up for the foreseeable future.

"I don't think, necessarily, we'll ever go back to the old ways," she said. "Food deliveries. Grocery deliveries. People finding new avenues to make money and things like that. Entrepreneurship has went up. Real estate has went up. So many other business avenues have went up during the coronavirus."

A mother of six in Los Angeles, she earned a real estate license during the year. She was also a director, scout and actress in show business. She was often away from home. Pre-pandemic, she was often outside the home working or seeking work. She was in Barstow for a play.

"During the last 15 months," she said, "I've been able to be the mother that I haven't been able to do in the past few years because of my lifestyle. The corona has brought closeness to my family again. Our family time. We've been doing all kind of stuff. Doing things as a family unit."

The last year made her think of her faith and the preciousness of life.

"I have a mindset that we are blessed every time we wake up," she said. "Every time we wake up, we have the opportunity to do something we didn't do the day before. And I believe that I am out here to change lives and help to grow to be the best person that they can be. I feel like I'm a vessel from God, one of his warriors to help his people."

Her eyes welled with tears and she chocked up when thinking about her friends in show business that passed away.

"I have lost a lot of people in the entertainment business," she said.

"So many artists passed away during the coronavirus. So I have felt the ugliness of the corona. I'm getting emotional right now."

When the interview ended, like lightning, her mood changed to exuberant. In her powder-blue cap and rose-colored glasses, she flashed a smile so big it was blinding.

A Three Percenter Loses 30 Friends

WEARING A BLACK SKI MASK, black shirt, and black vest, Tony Martin Blank was at the Barstow Walmart talking pandemic and American morals.

The attack on the US Capitol was just four months prior to the interview, and the Three Percenters were among the paramilitary groups participating. He did not mention if he participated in the capitol storming. He was a former mercenary who worked worldwide, employed by the controversial former private military services company Blackwater.

"I would like to go ahead and also to say 'Hi' to my friends in Blackwater and also the armed services," he said. "Thanking them for giving us that blanket of freedom that cost us so much … (later adding) And I'm asking the Three Percenters. Remember your oath. That means to protect the citizens over anybody else's decisions."

He was a caretaker for a non-biological "brother" who died of Covid. In total, he lost "about 30" friends to the disease.

Claiming to have special knowledge on vaccines, he said he did not intend to get a shot.

"I have a lot of friends in the medical field and in the army and disease control," he said. "And they told me that the vaccinations that they're giving out, unfortunately, are not proved.

"There are also fraud vaccinations. People are taking advantage. They're giving false shots. And stealing from those who need that shot. So that they're causing more problems over the initial shot. We see a lot of negative ramifications for a lot of people … because of the vaccination."

Originally from Pasadena, he was also an artist and musician.

He believed the government didn't do enough to protect people from the disease.

"There were poor people who were grateful for the assistance the government kindly went ahead and allotted," he said about the stimulus checks program.

He was "blessed with a child" during the year, and he worried for her "safety and her future." He got through on the strength of his "faith."

Americans should pull together and work for a better world.

"Life is precious, and it shouldn't be wasted," he said. "God bless everybody, and God bless America."

As the interview was winding up, he complimented me for seeking out stories found nowhere else. He was grateful to have his say and be seen.

"I'm really grateful for this gentleman (me) for coming out and doing these things because this is where the real stories come from and not illusions and not lies."

(*Author note: Martin's interview is much longer. It's recommended that it be viewed in full on* The Story Cycle *channel.*)

"It was apocalyptic" – says Hotel Clerk

ANGELO LOMBARDI WAS in the Walmart parking lot when he spotted my bicycle sign "Tell Me a Story."

He was uprooted early in the pandemic, mid-March 2020. He was hired by a Pasadena hotel but when California's pandemic restrictions kicked in, he was fired before he was hired.

So he packed up and moved to Barstow to be near his parents and worked nights as a front-desk attendant at Barstow Hotel.

He was experiencing "mask fatigue." He wore his mask at work but not when patrons were gone from the lobby. And he was vaccine hesitant.

"Not as of yet," he said of being vaccinated. "I plan to. I'm just kinda waiting to see if there are any long-term or short-term side-effects ... if any."

He worried about the speed at which the vaccines were created.

"I haven't really seen anyone since the whole thing started," he said of social distancing. "I have been keeping myself distant. I really just go out for work. Like right now, I'm just dropping off a movie at Redbox (at the Walmart). But I really just go from work and grocery shopping. The only reasons I leave the house. And then I really just hunker down."

He acknowledges that isolation from friends is affecting him.

"It has taken a toll," he said. "I like to be bike riding. I like to be outdoors. So I mean, it's affected me in that sense. It has gotten me down, you know. But I try to keep my spirits up by watching something funny on the internet or something."

He worried about his father's pre-existing conditions. Neither of his parents were vaccinated, but they social distanced by rarely leaving their house. He wasn't sure why they were hesitant too.

For him, the pandemic was a time for personal growth.

"It's helping me grow a little more," he said. "Because I'm more reliant on myself, in a sense, because I'm not mixing with anybody. My current happiness isn't relying on the group settings ... if I'm in a funk, (I think) how do I get myself out of this funk."

California's response to the pandemic was dramatic, he said, the empty streets made it look like the end of the world.

"When the initial lockdown happened, I was doing food deliveries out in the L.A. area," he said. "It was apocalyptic."

The pandemic, he thought, will have long lasting implications. The cryptocurrency trend will last, he predicted.

"I think certain aspects will stick around," he said. "The masking. I don't know that will stick around forever. But certain aspects of it, I believe, will stick around."

The pandemic strengthened his belief that you should "appreciate what you got."

"As soon as things settle down, don't worry about keeping up with the Joneses," he said. "And enjoy the small things."

Taco Stand Conspiracies in the High Desert

I MET William Marvin David at a taco stand in Oro Grande in the California High Desert.

He was taking no precautions and was convinced he was never getting Covid.

"Never had it," he said, "never will."

He didn't know anybody who had it. But he believed the death statistics "because that's the government."

No masks. No distancing. No vaccinations. The only way he will get Covid, he said, is if he vaccinates.

"Why for? I'm doing just fine right now," he said. "I don't need it. That's when you get it, when they vaccinate you. That's when they give it to you. When you get that shot."

He believed the G-5 technology developed in China was behind the Covid spread.

"That G-5 stuff, they can't control it," he said. "When the Chinese did something with it like that, they did something they can't control."

The government's response has been "too much" in regards to masking and vaccines.

He thought doctors were ginning up the diagnosis of Covid cases "so they get the money from the government."

Money is driving the narrative on Covid, he claimed. That's why he didn't change his habits during the year.

His anxiety level and personal happiness remained untouched.

He thought the mainstream news about Covid deaths was "a bunch of poop."

"The most important thing that Covid has done, in my opinion, is it has laid bare the tremendous inequity in American society and the failures of many of our systems, including our health system to, take care of our citizens."
— **Los Angeles-native Evan Spiegel, multi-billionaire founder of Snapchat.**

"Doctors of the world: Stop lying about the Coronavirus. The people needs absolute TRUTH."
— **A tweet by Ice Cube, Compton-born rapper who reportedly rejected a multi-million dollar movie deal due to its vaccination requirement.**

COVID CITY OF ANGELS

L.A. COVID STORY IN DEVELOPMENT

LONG TRACKING SHOT -
Focus centers on a far-off bicycle rider peddling on Interstate 15's
westbound shoulder in the San Bernardino Mountains.
SWITCH TO BIKE HELMET CAMERA -
A close-up of the rider's hands on the handlebar. Picking up downhill
speed, he lets out a banshee scream!
FOCUS ON ROAD AHEAD -
The Cajon Summit sign ahead reads, "6% Grade." The speeding
bicycle passes trucks. Bouncing camera action. Truck horns.
CUE THE SOUNDTRACK -
"Born to be Wild" - by Los Angeles - based Steppenwolf

J rode like a madman out of the mountains as if in my own
Hollywood movie.

I was hurtling through space and time into La-La Land. I raced
down the mountainside in a dream of acceptable risks.

Ahead lay the Greater Los Angeles area, pop. 18.5 million. The
metropolitan area is larger than four Route 66 states combined -
Missouri, Kansas, Oklahoma, and New Mexico.

As soon as possible, I veered off Interstate 15 into San Bernardino and the City of Los Angeles.

I stayed overnight in the Arts District and later in a seedy West Hollywood motel before riding to the symbolic end of Route 66 on the Santa Monica Pier.

On that bright, warm May afternoon on the pier, I not only reached the end of the road, I interviewed my 100th person.

Santa Monica Pier has a "life is a carnival" vibe, with a Ferris wheel, rollercoaster, and fast food. There were Covid distancing and masking signs along the pier, but people were there to forget the cares of the pandemic and enjoy themselves.

Behind the pier was Greater Los Angeles, where it's best not to forget the pandemic.

The homeless count in Los Angeles County rose to "north of 80,000" that year, according to the L.A. County Sheriff's Department. That's a homeless population larger than the entire population of Flagstaff.

The pandemic hit Greater Los Angeles hard. Minorities and lower-income groups were disproportionately affected. Some parts of Greater Los Angeles led the country in unemployment. The death rates in the poorer sections of L.A. were three times higher than in wealthier areas.

The scope of the pandemic is magnified in cities, as if it's not even the same virus in rural America. As of 2022, there have been 3.4 million cases of Covid in Los Angeles County alone.

The heartbreaking reality of L.A. looks like pure fiction at a lone gas station in Newkirk, New Mexico, population 12.

People weren't viewing the same pandemic.

I trained as a lifeguard when I was young, and my biggest fear was drowning with a panicked swimmer. Drowning people try to pull you both down.

I believe by listening and learning from each other we'll save ourselves in this and future pandemics.

The trip ended with a view of the vastness of the Pacific Ocean from the Santa Monica Pier. I was out of my head, ecstatic to be alive.

I'd interviewed 100 actors during my cinematic Route 66 ride, but there's no Hollywood ending.

There's just the ocean ahead and somewhere out there beyond the happy pier lurks another white whale of pandemic.

CUE THE SOUNDTRACK -
"Straight Outta Compton" by Los Angeles - based N.W.A.
MOVIE FINALE -
Fade to white.

"I'm not going to live in fear"

DOTTIE J. Jansma-Williams called herself a conservative who believed the pandemic response was "beyond ridiculous."

She was from Wrightwood, pop. 4,500, near the Fontana gas station we met.

She knew people who went 12 rounds with the disease. Some already had underlying health conditions and suffered the fallout from long-haul Covid.

"They're old, like me," she said.

She did not like how the government responded to those and other pandemic cases.

"I call it a lockdown," she said. "I know people have problems. And I do what I can to help. But it's gone beyond ridiculous. I don't think anything that's being done is really addressing the situation. I'm not going to live in fear. I have my house open. People visit me and whatever ... I'm a trail angel for the Pacific Coast Trail."

The Pacific Coast Trail was beginning to open up to hikers, and she was taking them in for the night.

"We didn't have any hikers last year," she said. "But this year I've already had four different parties who have stayed at my house. So that's great."

The vaccine was developed while President Trump was in office, and he was vaccinated. So I wondered what was stopping her from vaccinating.

"First of all," she said, "it's a drug that doesn't have a history. Secondly, I get allergic reactions to things. Like serious. Like anaphylaxis. I don't see the reason to put something in my body that I don't need. Okay?"

She equated the mRNA vaccine to the common flu shot she got years ago.

"They said take the flu shot. So for years, I never took the flu shot, never had the flu," she said. "I took it for two or three years because they said, 'You're old. You're supposed to do it.' I took it. Period. I haven't had the flu shot for five or six years. Never had the flu during that time. So I don't see putting something unknown into my body that's not necessary. I'm glad that President Trump fast-tracked the vaccine for people who want it. I'm all for people doing what they want to do."

When I saw her, she was picking up her preschool granddaughter. She masked up if she needed to go into stores, but she didn't like it. She played cards with a group of women, some of whom did not mask either.

The government's response to Covid, she believed, was "taking away our freedoms."

"America is where we have freedom of choice," she said. "And you can make stupid decisions. You can say stupid things in our country. And you're allowed to. I'm not going to take away the right of anyone to say anything, no matter how dumb it is. And I'm not going to force anybody to do anything because I think it's right."

Her anxiety didn't heighten during the pandemic. She has found some pandemic measures "annoying," like the temporary closing of her church.

"Of all the stupid things to close. A church?" she said. "We've had some challenges on that, but I've gone to some churches that were open."

She lived alone and worked online on her realtor business. It hurt business when she couldn't "take people in the car" to see homes.

She predicted the country will not take much more of the pandemic restrictions.

"I think people are going to rebel," she said. "I think they're going to say, 'Enough!' At the beginning, we all thought, all right, a few weeks. We can deal with this. Now we have the government trying to take over every part of our lives, and that is not America."

The upcoming pandemic rebellion will be non-violent, she predicted. She thought people on both sides of the political spectrum will object to the economic turmoil and the mounting federal debt.

"People's businesses are being destroyed," she said. "People's jobs. Plus, look now, everywhere you go, 'Help Wanted' signs. Why? They sent me checks and cards I never asked for. I opened an account for my granddaughter. She and her kids are going to be paying for all that."

Her views on pandemic restrictions relied heavily on her religious faith.

"I'm not going to live in fear," she said. "I know who's in charge, and thank God it ain't us. So the good Lord has his hand on all human affairs. He works it out for his plan. It's gonna work out. So I'm not worried about anything. I don't worry about dying. I don't worry about anything. Because I know who is in charge."

She cited God and patriotism as reasons for opposing pandemic restrictions.

"I'm always protected and provided for by my good Father," she said. "M faith is my life. So I'm not worried about anything. Do you know how many times it says in the Bible 'do not fear'? That is the most thing (said). Okay?"

God and the US constitution guided her.

"I'm not going to be afraid," she said. "Whatever it is, it'll work out. And so I don't feel I'm any more particularly protected than anybody else. The one person I knew who died was a very great man of faith. So I don't know how God thinks. His ways are not our ways. His thoughts are not our thoughts. But I am comfortable with my life.

"And I'm not going to roll over and play dead for people trying to take away our American rights and our constitution."

"I have angels protecting me"

A FOUR-YEAR VETERAN retailer at the Hollywood Farmer's Market, David Oredugba remembered the pre-pandemic market dynamics.

"It definitely was an adjustment, but it also was a blessing as well," he said. "It gave time to put things in perspective, figure out, ya know, life and what I'm doing."

Along with this brother, he owned NYA (as in Not Your Average Tea), and he believed tea helped people during the Covid times.

"We've been able to kinda give people solace, especially during a time of confusion and health worries. And a lot of unknowns. Tea is one of those daily rituals of comfort that, we discovered from our clients, gave people a sense of calm. That was really rewarding."

He said he was taking all the precautions. He masked-up, distanced, and vaccinated. His father "works in medicine" and was vaccinated. He felt he had to vaccinate to travel and be with his family. But he understood people who had "apprehensions and don't want to take it."

It sounded like he felt less protected by the vaccination than by his faith.

"As a Christian, I feel like I have angels protecting me and that whatever outcome of the situation happens ... happens," he said. "Right now, I'm using faith to protect me."

Isolation and distancing, he said, have their good sides. He turned to cat apps and Club House to create social circles and "fill a social void."

"This was a paradigm shift," he said. "I think the world kinda needed this in a sort of way. I'm not saying (the world needed) the downsides or the death. I mean, it kinda forced us to reset."

Outside the tea business, he expanded into a cryptocurrency investment. He thought the pandemic taught people to be less dominated by a central authority.

"People can take ownership of their health if they want to vaccine or distance," he said. "People can take ownership of their wealth if they want to put their money into a more sound financial asset that's controlled by the people, which is Bitcoin. I think people have had to ask themselves, 'What is my place in this new world?' I mean, we are in a new world that is changing, and the conversation is, 'What is my role in this new utopia?'"

He predicted that bio-hacking and bio-privacy would become the "new thing," along with the rise of bioethics.

"It's kinda hard to trust nations that have lied before," he said. "If you ask the Indians. If you ask the Black Tuskegee experiment (who unwittingly participated in a syphilis study). If you ask different marginalized groups. But you have to trust and live."

As for his view on life, the pandemic reaffirmed his belief in life.

"You gotta realize the beauty of social interaction - friends and family. Ya know, you gotta live," he said

"I know people will agree and disagree, but fuck-it, you gotta live," he said. "It is what it is. That's my philosophy. Live to the beat of your drum. Live to the beat of your truth. And live to create. Live to love. Live to fuck up. Live to give. Just live, ya know what I mean?"

Selling Healthy from the Granola Tent

ATHENA ARAMOVICH WAS SELLING healthy granola at the Hollywood Farmer's Market yet worried what "healthy" really means in a pandemic.

She masked, distanced and vaccinated as recommended. But she was still unsure how healthy the vaccinations are.

"My concerns were, I think like a lot of other people, that the vaccines were developed rather quickly," she said. "The other thing is we haven't had years to see how the side effects work. How the vaccine interacts with your body. If it's going to cause an autoimmune disorder, or whatever. I'm not a doctor, but of course, I have got those concerns."

Social pressures convinced her to conform to CDC advice despite her strong concerns.

"Most of my friends and family members have had the vaccine, and so, I talked it over with them," she said. "I told them I'm a bit concerned, but they tried to alleviate my concerns. Also, I'm at the farmers market and interacting with a lot of people. So I just want to feel like if I do contract Covid, which I hope I don't, it will lessen the effects and help me out that way."

She also sells granola and healthy living from her tent. She wished the government's pandemic response was more focused on total health as a way of fighting Covid.

"I just feel like during the pandemic, there was a lost opportunity to also tell people to take this time to really get yourself in shape," she said. "Eat well. Get lots of rest. Drink lots of water. Instead, (the message) was just - stay socially distanced and wear a mask."

She worried about the "mental health" of the elderly people in her family. Isolation kept them from being with their children and hugging their grandchildren.

"Thank golly for Zoom, and all the others, Skype, that allow the opportunity to see each other," she said. "Just to be able to (say) 'Oh, how are you? You look good.' You know, that kinda thing."

On a personal level, the pandemic had its good aspects too. She loved spending more time with her husband. She was there for the last year of her dog's life. And she learned to "appreciate things more."

"My husband and I have been lucky, because we were healthy," she said. "I had time to go out and garden ... It allowed me time to think about what is really, truly important - you know, family. And just making the most of the time that you're here because I feel like I blink my eyes and, you know ... (at my age) ... oh my gosh, where did the time go?"

As for the future, she feels "we are going to have a vaccinated future."

She wanted to see people in the food service business continue to mask. She had been to Japan, where everyday masking seemed normal to them.

Looking back on the year, she was grateful for her own health and sorry for the losses of others.

"It's been interesting," she said, "but I've been able to roll through it. I'm just glad I'm here. And I'm glad my health is intact. And I'm so sorry for the loss of life that occurred over the pandemic and continues to happen."

"I'm a stronger person"

JAMES GORDON WAS an Uber driver who talked to his customers about Covid.

"Most of my riders are on board with the current (Biden) administration," he said. "We're in a sort of more liberal area in the Santa Monica area. I think we're seeing a little bit of the light at the end of the tunnel. After a long dark year. People are more excited now."

I met Gordon in Santa Monica. He'd been driving an Uber for the last year. Before that, he worked in Berlin's film industry for six years.

He returned to America to help with his ailing mother, who was dying of cancer. When she passed away during the year, he was unable to travel to back Germany due to pandemic travel restrictions.

"That (Berlin) is where I'm comfortable living and where I want to spend the rest of my life," he said.

He vaccinated, wore an N-94 mask, and checked customer temperatures. He credited his precautions for being Covid-free all year.

"I think masking was very important, and critical," he said. "I don't think we got (Covid) from touching things nearly as much as (airborne)."

Anti-vaxxers and the vaccine-resistant didn't make sense to him.

"People who have a problem with (Covid vaccination), have already been vaccinated for everything from diphtheria, whooping cough, all these things you get. Polio. Measles. Rubella. All these things, they've already had the vaccination.

"So how can you argue, 'Oh I'm going to wait for a while to see if this works out'? Well fine. I think Darwinism will win out. And they'll eventually get sick, and they'll be properly vaccinated their own way."

He kept in touch with his Berlin friends through WhatsApp but was "really stressed out."

"I come home from work, I don't have my mother to speak to anymore because she's passed," he said. "I don't have any friends because of the timing. I can only speak once or twice a week to Berlin because of it's a nine-hour difference."

He was exercising and running more "to get rid of the Covid belly but also to help with the stress."

The pandemic called on him to drive an Uber car for a year while living in temporary housing, including a bunk-room hotel and Airbnb.

"I've learned how much I really enjoyed living in Berlin," he said. "I think I'm a stronger person than I would be for having done this. I've been driving an Uber for a year, which is insane. I never thought I was capable of doing that."

The pandemic sparked his philosophical side.

"I think we've learned how important relationships are," he said. "I think we've learned how important it is where we are. And I think we've learned what's not important in our lives. I think we're all going to be better out of this. The deck got reshuffled. And in some ways, I think we have to look at what's good that has come out of this. And then we go from there."

He sensed more "competence" in the Biden administration. And he predicted an "explosion of vaccinations" and a willingness to get vaccinated.

"I think the boat has been turned around," he said. "And I think we have an interesting future ahead of us."

Customers told him they had a pent-up desire to "get back to normal."

"We're a social animal, and there's only so much we can take before we start really taking risks to get back to where we were," he said. "'Okay, we can do this for a while.' And then we'll start taking risks because we so much desire to have things the way they were. It's an alien feeling not to be able to go do things we want to do. I think we'll find a happy medium. We'll keep people safe, and we'll allow ourselves our freedoms. It's a slow process, but I think we'll work it out just fine."

He finished the interview with a quote from one of his favorite politicians.

"Churchill once said, 'Americans wait to the very last minute to do the right thing, but then they do.'"

"I have huge anxieties"

LORAN JAMES'S information loop told him the vaccine was to be more feared than the disease.

The Los Angeles native was a certified nursing assistant providing personal care for the elderly and those with autism. He regularly advised on vaccines but was worried the shots were killers.

"One guy was hospitalized for a month," he said of a patient who got the Covid vaccination. "He either got a blood clot at the same time or … They're saying that it wasn't from Covid. But recently, we're hearing about the blood clots. Most likely, it was from it. Just my opinion."

James speculated that a male patient he never met suffered blood clots because of vaccine shots, even though he heard just the opposite.

He was referencing news reports that several women suffered blood clots from the Johnson & Johnson vaccine, which led to a temporary suspension of the vaccine for further study. The reports cautioned that the clots were rare and found only in women under 50.

A Black CNA working with the elderly, James fell into two vaccine-hesitant groups.

CNAs, particularly those serving the elderly, were among the most vaccine hesitant in the early days of the rollout. A March 2021 survey by the CDC showed less than half of nursing home workers were vaccinated.

At the same time, several studies showed vaccine hesitancy was higher among African Americans and so too were hospitalizations and fatalities.

James said his worries stemmed from the experiences and opinions of his colleagues, many of whom reported bad outcomes from vaccines.

He was hearing one thing from the CDC and the opposite advice from friends.

Masking and distancing made sense to him, but cases like the J&J blood clot cases convinced him to resist vaccination.

His employer tested him bi-weekly. Daily and weekly tests weren't being offered.

He did not want to get a vaccination "until I get a little more educated." He was unsure of his medical coverage. And he feared the contents of the shot.

"My fear is, I don't mind taking it, but if anything happens, will they cover for me?" he said. "Are they going to do everything in their power to care for me - which I don't know about that. And I don't know too much information about what's in the shot."

He never took pills when sick, he said. Even Tylenol made him ill.

"Just imagine taking a shot," he said. "I don't know how my body would take that. So there's a fear of that."

Other healthcare workers, he said, were the ones warning him about vaccinations.

"Probably like, I met a few, maybe 50 percent of them had some horrible outbreaks," he said. "One of my friend's girlfriend, she had to be rushed to the hospital. She couldn't breathe ... that was first shot. She took the first shot, she had to be rushed to the hospital. She's okay now. And she's a nurse."

With 50 percent of his friends having "horrible outbreaks," little wonder he was hesitant.

"But I know a few people had blood clots," he said. "A few people have died, just what I heard. And on the TV, they'll pretty much give you a certain amount of numbers of (people who) passed."

The pandemic supercharged his anxieties.

"I have huge anxieties (when) I never had anxieties before," he said. "Just not being around family. And life in general. So I think it was a little too much for me. I'm a little older, so you get more sensitive. And you get older, and you try not to take days for granted. For some reason, it kicked in a big anxiety for me."

He was adapting with prayer and "getting myself out there online." He tried to talk to his family "more and more about anxiety and just being open with it because it wasn't a huge thing in my life until last year."

His pandemic hobbies were music, diet, and exercise. And "I've really been putting my health on check."

His top priority, though, has been "fighting anxieties (and) trying to do something I love to do."

He was no fan of the national response to Covid and was surprised by the divisiveness.

"Too many divisions," he said. "Too many back-and-forths. In a crisis like this, you would think everybody would join together, even the government, even their parties. I don't see none of that. So it gets you even more worried. At the same time, you rely on your faith and pray."

When asked about the future of Covid, he relied on his understanding of Biblical teachings.

"I go off of what God explains how the world's going to be," he said. "It's going to get worse. Man is not capable of making peace. In the Bible, it says that."

Overall, he pleaded for everyone to work at staying healthy and grateful for life.

"Please don't take days for granted," he said. "Your health is your bread and butter. Your health is your everything. Everything can be going so great in your life, soon as your health comes, or something bad happens to you, nothing else matters in your life. It's about your health.

"Get more educated on health. Get more educated on where you're taking your body. Stay away from hate, that causes stress. Learn to love. If you're not able to, ask. Do your research. Get together with people. Be positive."

Hollywood Agent Talks Alternative Cure

MIKE GREENFIELD WAS a semi-retired Hollywood agent who believed he knew of a Covid cure not yet federally approved and as yet undiscovered by the media.

He first heard about it from a friend.

"The first person I knew (who contracted Covid) almost died the first month," he said. "And she got saved by a cure that exists. Obviously, the cure has been stifled by the pharmaceutical army around the world, but it's about to get out."

A native of Los Angeles, Greenfield was once the agent for some of the biggest stars in Hollywood and was still active in the entertainment industry. He agreed to meet me at the renowned Jewish deli Nate 'n Al's in Beverly Hills.

The cure was developed for another virus several years ago, he said, and now was being applied to Covid.

"It was invented about 20-some years ago, actually for (another) virus," he said. "And all of a sudden when this Covid hit, they tried it on this virus, and it's worked miracles. I have eight people that I know of, personally - everyone had Covid bad - and every one of them survived and got rid of Covid. Very quickly. Quicker than you can get rid of a cold. And everyone I know recovered very fast. I mean one day. It's not out yet."

The undisclosed drug, he said worked for his friend.

"I knew about it through the most unusual circumstances," he said. "I have a casting director who will actually cast our project, who is a person I've known for, I guess, three decades, and she did something interesting.

"She was dying. She could hardly breathe. And she somehow decided to put out the fact that she was dying out on the internet. I don't know if that's the smartest thing to do, but she did. And got called by a woman who had been a publicist in show business, previously four years earlier. (Her friend) called her and said, 'I'm going to send you something, and you're going to get cured immediately.'"

His friend was so desperate for something to save her life that she listened to her friend's medical advice.

"And (she said) 'I don't care if you give me salami - anything that will help me because I am dying. And I prefer not to die.' At the time, I think she was 59 or 60. I first found out about it because I was friends with her, and was feeling really bad. I was about to lose a friend. She got it so bad ... Anyway, the cure has been very effective for the people fortunate enough to have used it."

I asked for the name of the drug, but he was not sure of the drug or the drug company developing it.

"I don't know the name of it," he said. "It doesn't really have a name. In San Francisco, their factory is there ... The elements (of the drug) were approved last year, in July, by the FDA. ... It was supposed to be tested at the Cleveland Clinic in Ohio. I'm sure you know who they are. For some reason, this never got done. They never were actually able to do the tests on it."

Greenfield wasn't vaccinated yet for two reasons. His appointment to get the Johnson & Johnson vaccination was delayed because there was a national pause in delivering it. Also, he had friends who had bad reactions to their vaccinations.

"I know people who had a really bad reaction. I'd say about half the people had some kind of reaction. A very serious reaction."

He masked and socially distanced when he could.

"First of all, I live alone," he said. "I have not had any social gatherings. There was one. But basically, most of the people I've known have had situations with it (vaccines), and they're pretty much at the point where they know that I'm healthy. And I've been tested."

He was critical of the government's response.

"Do I think the first response was good? No," he said. "It was terrible. Forget about the seriousness of it because nobody knew the seriousness of it. Even to this day it is questionable. How serious is it long-term? When 550,000 people die, that's a sizable amount. But if you look at the world population, that's not much. However, the death rate around the world is out of hand."

He was hesitant to say what the future of Covid holds. He worried that vaccinations might cause some long-term ill effects.

"I think we'll be vaccinating for a while," he said. "And I question the vaccinations that came up so quick. To the level of long-term, I don't know. I don't think anybody knows. Everybody's got an opinion. Most people aren't qualified."

Sometimes during the pandemic, he asked what life was all about.

"I was in bad trouble," he said. "I was seriously wondering what life was going to be about."

The pandemic changed the trajectory of his life.

"You want to know what the tragedy of all this is? It's taken a year and a half of our lives," he said. "I could've done many different things. Do I see any good that came out of it, no, ... this country is the most divided since it's been since the Civil War. I sit in wonderment of how this empire is falling apart."

Overall, he managed to stay healthy and busy in the entertainment field.

"I'm probably busier now than I've been in many years," he said. "The fact that I feel good is best of all, and I lost a lot of weight."

"Life is a random walk to begin with"

STEVE PARKES HAPPENED BY NATE N' AL's deli in Beverly Hills by chance and took a seat when he saw his lifelong friend Mike Greenfield.

A resident of Century City, he talked about the fickleness of life in general and how that amps up in a pandemic.

He vaccinated and reluctantly masked. But he saw family and "most of my friends fairly regularly without much of a disruption."

Although the pandemic did not upend his personal life, his real estate business needed managing.

"I virtually had no anxiety," he said. "The only disruptions were what the government required in the way of disruptions."

He thought California's response to the pandemic was "over the top."

"I think they bankrupted a lot of small businesses in the state unnecessarily," he said. "What's the difference if three or four people are in a small store at one time? Or even two, for that matter? They basically forced businesses out of business."

Income from his properties was down by half.

"Personally, of all the buildings I have an interest in, our income is down over 50 percent," he said. "And a lot of it has to do with the overreach of the government, particularly the city of West Hollywood - which basically gave all the tenants a (rental) moratorium - which is still in effect ... in other words, a tenant can just pay whatever they feel like."

Despite the challenges, he was not going to be a pandemic casualty.

"Mainly because the properties are all free and clear," he said. "It didn't affect my life that much. I have other activities in other states. They were doing just fine. That offset those losses."

His personal life took a blow when he separated from his wife, and he needed his friendships to sustain him during the pandemic.

A self-described conservative, he worried that the pandemic was allowing the American government to grab more power over individuals.

"I think Covid opened the door for more government regulation," he said. "Not just about disease control, but our overall regulation of people. How they operate. Where they go, And what they do. The biggest event, in my opinion, wasn't the pandemic. It was the ability of the government to influence and intercede in our lives. And I think that's something that won't disappear anytime soon."

He thinks it was mostly "luck" that he didn't get Covid.

"Let's face it, life is a random walk to begin with," he said. "Getting Covid is sort of really a random thing. It all depends on your immune system, and none of us really knows what our immune system is and how we have the ability to fight off disease.

"I mean, you could get cancer just as easily as you could get Covid. They still don't know how one gets cancer."

"I actually cried"

DAVID LEIF & Marcia Castonguey stopped along the famed shopping district along Rodeo Drive in Beverly Hills to speak about their experiences with Covid.

Both from Southern California, they were shopping while vaccinated and masked.

"We've been very careful this year. I did go out a lot," Marcia Castonguey said. "Once we got vaccinated, we got together. He (pointing to David Leif) is my son-in-law. So I can hug my grandkids again. So that's good. And we're out doing more stuff now."

Leif had been socially distancing but easing up since his vaccination. His immediate family has been quarantining "together" with "a couple of families."

Castonguey kept life interesting by exercising and "a lot of FaceTime."

"It hasn't been that rough on me," she said. "I know that some people have suffered more than I have. Maybe it's my personality or my DNA, but I've been okay."

Castonquey was clearing the house and gardening during the year.

"A lot of stuff has gotten done because I was forced to stay at home," she said.

Leif agreed.

"I had a little bit of anxiety for my children, not getting out there and being able to do things," Leif said. "But other than that, for the most part, no, no real anxiety."

The pandemic gave Lief more time for family.

"I got a little bit closer with my kids," he said, "a little bit closer with my family. And even though we may not have been seeing everybody, we were talking and FaceTiming and Zooming. And had some good laughs and made the best of the situation."

As for anything good happening during the year, Castonquey was cleaning up around the house and gardening more. Leif was getting "a little bit closer to my family."

Castonquey felt like getting the vaccine was tantamount to saving her life.

"When I got it, I actually cried," she said. "Because I felt so relieved. Because I thought, 'Okay, I'm not going to die if I get it.'"

She didn't think the government's response to the pandemic was enough.

"They should have listened to the scientists," she said. "They should have shut us down sooner. You know, taken control."

Leif had "mixed feelings" about the government's response.

"I think in some respects, I think our local governments reacted properly," he said, "and in some respects they didn't."

He was worried about being vaccinated.

"I (vaccinated) out of respect for a lot of people," he said. "To keep other people safe as well, but it's a new vaccine. And it's that new and untested. I had some reservations."

Both of them had positive life philosophies they wanted to share.

"Live every day to the fullest," Leif said. "Tell your loved ones that you love them. You don't know what tomorrow will bring."

Castonguey agreed.

"Have a positive attitude," she said. "It is what it is. Deal with it."

Leif chimed in, "and don't complain."

"Yeah," Castonquey said, "we're all in this together."

Solitude of a UCLA Cognitive Science Major

ANDREW SKROBAK WAS a UCLA student grateful to the pandemic for the gift of solitude.

"There was a lot of good stuff that happened," he said. "Mainly in the way of, like, solitude. Being able to slow down and think about (things). I feel like I'm at a fork in my life."

Andrew Skrobak was a cognitive science major at UCLA. He masked, socially distanced and vaccinated. Most of his friends are "pretty fine with" vaccinating too.

He had his doubts about vaccination but said he did it for others.

"For my sake, too, but mostly for other people around me, in terms of comfort," he said. "As long as I'm healthy, I'm doing everything that I can, in terms of vitamins and stuff like that ... I just think about being cautious, I guess."

He thought some of the city's pandemic policies were "illogical," but he credits people with good intentions.

"I think everyone was trying to make the best, most responsible decision possible, so I'm not upset or anything," he said. "But I definitely would have liked to see it be more logical ... in terms of outdoor dining and small business closures.

"And, like, PPE, I don't think was fairly distributed ... I also like to kinda stay out of that sort of thing because it's a little bit complex."

The pandemic changed his college experience. All his classes were online. He spent more time with his roommates doing Southern California "stuff."

"There have been, like, pods of people that usually spend time together," he said. "There's a popular hill called Janss Steps that people go to and watch the sunset, so people usually meet up over there. I know frats that definitely had their own new pledge classes and everything throughout this year ... I mostly spent the year just with my roommates, hiking, biking, beach. Stuff like that."

As for his own mental well-being, his car helped him cope.

"I've been able to drive back (home) three times since September, during Thanksgiving, Christmas, and one other time just for fun," he said. "But in terms of anxiety, I really like my roommates. They're my best friends. So we've been able to spend a lot of time together."

He credits his time alone as being a learning experience. He went places, volunteered, and read books on his own.

"Just time alone," he said. "I think about the things I want to do. It's definitely different than, like, being in college and being able to throw yourself into any situation you want. And then figure yourself out that way.

"But I've equally had an enjoyable experience, like, really sitting down and reading a lot of books I wouldn't have otherwise read. Or going places. I started volunteering at the farmers market in Santa Monica. I met a lot of people that way, which I probably never would have done because I'd always have been hungover."

His solitude has led to some meta-analysis of himself, which he tries to limit.

"I rethought the fundamental principles of certain things," he said. "But I think that trying to meta-analyze myself too much would probably be a little destructive, so I try to avoid that. Just knowing myself."

First Pandemic Vacation

WALKING ALONG SANTA MONICA PIER, New Orleans native Patrick Crochet was on his first pandemic vacation.

"I do mask, and I am vaccinated," he said, "but it's not mandatory where I come from. We spend a lot of time in Mississippi. We have a home there, and nobody wears a mask there. I can go to Home Depot and Lowe's and places like that in New Orleans, and nobody has a mask over there either."

He was uncertain about the effectiveness of masking.

"I'm not an anti-masker, but I don't know that it's necessary," he said. "I don't know when it's going to stop. But sometimes, yes, I think it's over-done."

He was more certain about vaccines.

"I've had the vaccination, and I think that's a good idea, and I think everybody should get the vaccine."

His family didn't mask or distance. From Santa Monica, they were on to the Hawaii leg of their vacation.

"When our family gets together, nobody has a mask on," he said. "We have family that's close by, and we're always together."

Overall, his lifestyle has been affected "none whatsoever."

As for the future, he adopted a positive point of view.

"I think eventually," he said, "within the next year, it's going to die out."

He wasn't sure why he and his family had escaped the ravages of the pandemic so far.

"I don't know the reason why I've survived or why nobody we know has had it," he said. "Maybe it's because of where we live. Maybe it's not prevalent in the New Orleans area like it is in some other parts of the country. I just hope that in the near future, we don't see much of it. And hopefully, it's going to go away."

"We Learned to Love Living"

BEING FROM TURKEY, Alican Erol saw how L.A.'s pandemic response differed from Istanbul's lockdown.

We met on Santa Monica Pier. He said Istanbul and L.A. were worlds apart in their reaction to the pandemic.

"Life is difficult, you know. It's really tough," he said. "Why? Now (in L.A.) I can drink something, and I can eat something on the outside or on the inside. But if I'm in Turkey now, I cannot eat because all the restaurants and all the shopping malls are closed. All the offices are closed, so I work at home. I don't know anything about when I'll see again my friends."

His anxiety rose as life became more difficult.

"Yeah, it's tough," he said. "Because for example, if you need to print something but you don't have a printer, you have to go to the office and then go back to home. Because after 7 p.m. all the roads are closed you cannot go outside. You should not walk. Just grocery stores. Just the pharmacy. That's it. The situation is not good. There's a lockdown."

He believed that humans are social animals and we need each other to be happy.

"What happened is tough because people are happy with social things. Drink something with your friends. Eat something with your friends, and that's it. So it's tough for me. I'm a social guy, you know."

Before the pandemic, he loved socializing, running, shopping, and drinking. Since the pandemic, he learned to slow down.

"I learned how to stay home," he said. "I learned (to take life) slowly."

He thinks it will be 2023, at least, before 60 to 70 percent of the world is vaccinated and back to normal. But the future will never be "100 percent" normal again. Maybe "96 percent," but the world has changed.

He got one vaccination and is waiting for the second dose.

Comparing the US to Turkey, he believed the US was better at vaccinating people, but Turkey was better at primary care and masking.

"Look at this (pier)," he said. "Everyone's kissing. Talking ... a little bit dangerous maybe."

The pandemic taught him something about life.

"We learned to love living," he said. "Before Covid, I don't know anything about that. Because I was not close (to death). But now I'm close. Maybe I'll (get) Covid and I'll pass away.

"So I learned something. We have to see the advantage. If we see always the disadvantage, we cannot be happy. I'm good."

Pilot and Pregnant Wife Fear Vaccine More

JON AND DANIELLE SHAFFER were professionals who decided not to mask, distance or vaccinate because she was pregnant. They feared the cure might be worse than the disease.

Danielle Shaffer was a nurse, and Jon was a pilot. They were "waiting" before deciding on vaccinations.

"We don't have any research on pregnancy stuff," Jon Shaffer said of Danielle's decision not to vaccinate. "I'm waiting on it, due to the FAA ... I'm not sure what their requirements will be on that."

They wanted the vaccines to go through the whole FDA approval process before they got their shots.

"If things continue to go as well as they have now, I have no problem getting the vaccine," Jon Shaffer said. "As of now, we're waiting for the approval to go through."

They were also deeply concerned about family members at high risk.

"I have an 84-year-old grandmother who is at high risk, and we kept our distance around her," Danielle Shaffer said. "She's fully vaccinated now. Most of our family is fully vaccinated. We kept our circle small during the higher times."

When asked about the government's response to the pandemic, Jon Shaffer said the federal government was overreaching.

"For me personally, I don't think the federal government, generally, should be telling me how to live my life, what's best for me," Jon Shaffer said. "I think I know a little bit more what's good for me than other people."

Jon Shaffer thought widespread business shutdowns was wrong.

"I certainly know better than the federal government what's good for my life," Jon Shaffer said. "But again, I'm reasonable, it's a virus, and masks are going to help that, but I don't think shutting down our whole world, for something with such a high survivability rate, was the right move."

When I asked if anything good happened during the pandemic, they eagerly shook their heads yes.

"We got pregnant," Jon Shaffer said.

"Got to be home more," Danielle Shaffer agreed. "We got to spend more time, quality time, with family and friends, that's for sure. It makes you appreciate things."

They said they grew to appreciate what they have during the year.

"If you can take the good from any situation, it could be the worst situation in the world, you can learn from it," Jon Shaffer said. "Learn to appreciate the good."

It's a was disastrous first year of the pandemic, he said, but it was difficult to say what the right thing to do was.

"I think it's a little too early for me to come up with a philosophical (point of view) on the issue. It's such a complicated issue," he said. "We probably saved a lot of lives by shutting down things, but you've also destroyed a lot of lives by shutting down things ... So it's so complicated it's really hard to nail down ... I think overall, it's been an absolute disaster, of course."

Danielle Shaffer chimed in, saying that it was a mess for the economy and small businesses.

"There were so many mixed messages," she said. "Once we got a little more educated on it, got more of a handle on things, how it spread, that young healthy people generally can recover okay (she knew more)."

However, the more she educated herself on Covid, the more she saw the need to keep the "immunocompromised safe and people at higher risk safe. There's a middle ground there."

As for the future, Jon Shaffer thought "liberal" areas will keep their masks for a long time, and places like Utah will not.

"It depends," he said, "on where you are."

Pandemic Life

"We're terrible animals. I think that the Earth's immune
system is trying to get rid of us, as well it should."
— **Kurt Vonnegut, author of Galapagos, a comic/pandemic
novel set a million years in the future when humans must evolve
into human seals, with blubber, fur, and smaller brains.**

"In 1736, I lost one of my sons, a fine boy of four years old,
by the smallpox in the common way. I long regretted
bitterly and still regret that I had not given it to him by
inoculation."
— **Ben Franklin's regret. Inoculation meant giving smallpox to
healthy patients, producing a mild case, thereby vastly reducing
the risk of death.**

SPIRIT OF A PANDEMIC

ORDINARY PEOPLE IN EXTRAORDINARY TIMES

I do have insights from a long, slow journey with an open mind.

Without exception, everyone spoke of helping and loving others.

It was the single deepest lesson of the pandemic, most people said. People found the closeness of death made them more grateful for life.

"I think making people more aware of loving each other and being close to each other because you never know how much longer somebody can truly be around. I think that's a good thing that came from this," said Marine Tyler Reich in Yukon, Oklahoma.

People started out talking about the disease and moved on to talk about what makes life worth living.

The best discoveries I made along the way were counterintuitive.

Most people were optimistic and mostly happy. Arron Eskam, of Norman, Oklahoma, said a mix of altruism and family made his pandemic life a ten out of ten.

It took me a while before I began to see the pattern. A significant group of people wanted to change their lives and the pandemic was their chance.

People discovered new sides of themselves, taking up hobbies and starting up their dream business.

I heard people say they hated the slow death of the office. Working from home brightened their lives.

The more I listened, the more I heard about income inequality, racial discrimination and flaws in the American healthcare system.

Andrew Sega was a shy African American teen working the Walmart parking lot in Barstow, California. I reminded him that he was more than a low-wage shopping cart collector. He was part of all this, I told him, and people need to hear what he thinks.

He talked of being afraid of vaccines because he didn't know enough about them. He feared the growing isolation of his generation.

Sega was worth listening to and completely invisible to the national discussion.

Galen Pinto was a resident of the Navajo Nation and pissed off about the pandemic wiping out so many of his family and friends. He jumped at the chance to say racism, poverty and neglect are killers too.

"A lot of Navajos in the Navajo Nation don't even have (drinkable, running) water," he said, when we met in Gallup, New Mexico. "They can't even get to the hospitals."

The proliferation of conspiracy theories blew me away. I kept hearing more as I rode. I noticed that many conspiracy theorists seemed to have a mental illness, and several acknowledged suffering from depression.

Conspiracy theories are linked to mental health issues. There must be a connection to the mental health crisis in America.

Upwards of 20 percent of our nation lives with a severe form of mental illness, about 10 million, according to the National Institutes of Mental Health.

What does it mean that our national leadership was so unprepared for the pandemic that so many vulnerable people were rudderless and left adrift?

It's always been that way. Every pandemic has brought with it secret cures, charlatans, and far-fetched theories.

With Covid, the partisan media outlets found doctors to refute mainstream science. They pointed out times when mainstream medicine was colossally wrong at times in the past.

The ancient Greek physician Hippocrates once said, "Listen to the doctor but make up your own mind."

Rancher Jerry Spitz in Canute, Oklahoma, made up his own mind when he was turned away by the emergency room in the next town over. He went to his barn and took the cattle dewormer Ivermectin and a livestock steroid.

He survived Covid and credited Ivermectin, even though the drug has repeatedly been proven ineffective. The steroid has shown some efficacy but can kill if taken in the wrong dose.

Spitz worried about drug companies, greedy doctors, Ivermectin, hydroxychloroquine, socialists, Microsoft billionaire Bill Gates, Dr. Fauci, and Chinese chemical warfare. He expressed his fears while his voice cracked and tears welled in his eyes.

As hard as it is to believe, he wasn't all wrong. The Ivermectin dewormed him, he later found a worm in his toilet. The steroid may have strengthened his breathing when he felt death was seconds away. He was alive. At least the last time I saw him.

Spitz was worth saving too. He told funny, affectionate family and ranching stories. I met his father, who told a risqué joke and laughed hardest of all. Acts of kindness and generosity were among his favorite topics. He seemed like a thoroughly good, intelligent man living in a time that tested him to the edge of his limits.

I heard too many people express skepticism about public health institutions such as the Centers for Disease Control, which they considered to be "political." They believed more in their friends, their "own research," partisan media, and skeptical political influencers.

When not vaccinating or masking, they linked their response to being conservative, God-fearing and/or loyal to former President Trump. They cited TV, internet and doctor friends.

They weren't all wrong either.

Distrust in government medical information during the 1918 flu pandemic was justified. The US government publicly underestimated the severity of the flu in an attempt to manage perceptions during

World War I. Many in the media followed suit, due to institutional bias and a sense of patriotism.

The CDC admits to mistakes during the first year of Covid and is reforming but it was overwhelmingly correct on the measure that saved the most lives — vaccines.

The majority of people along America's Main Street told me they believed the CDC on Covid. Most people across the country are vaccinated, and when asked, they masked-up and distanced.

True to my Chicago area roots, I interviewed the owner of my favorite pizzeria at the beginning and end of the trip. Tom Dioguardi of Primo Pizza in Barrington owned the pizzeria I worked for when I was 15-years-old. A genius of crust and sauce is a man to be trusted.

Before I left on the ride, Dioguardi feared he might have to shut down if a single staff member caught Covid. When I came back, he feared having too few employees.

"Now, no one wants to work," he said. "I have a help wanted sign out there, and I haven't had one out there in 12 years. I can't find help."

He blamed the $15 trillion federal relief package aimed at thwarting the greatest economic crisis since the Great Depression. Dioguardi believed extended unemployment benefits kept people at home.

I believe he was partly right, but people changed during the pandemic.

More people are asking themselves the big questions in life.

They are reassessing their work and home lives. There's a reshuffling of the workforce touched off by Covid.

Going unspoken were the overarching dynamics of climate change and the Information Age.

Climate change is increasing the interactions between humans and other animals. People are encroaching on once wild land, making zoological viruses more likely to make the jump from other animals to people, making frequent pandemics more likely. Severe weather swings add to the uncertainty of the times.

The Information Age is both helping and disorienting people in a time when consensus is more important than ever. Vaccines were invented and rolled out like modern-day miracles. Yet the internet and partisan media undermined the trust in the news and science.

I began the Route 66 ride when vaccines were first introduced. As of early 2022, there were more than 300,000 excess deaths in America due to a lack of Covid vaccinations, according to a study by Brown University and Microsoft AI Health.

Multiply those 300,000-plus deaths by ten, grief experts say, and that's roughly how many people are actively grieving those lost souls.

We can't expect people to hold enlightened opinions if a person's external inputs don't overwhelmingly favor the enlightened.

The human brain consists of neurons and synapses being acted upon by internal and external forces. Nature and nurture. Logical fallacies. Cognitive biases. Life experiences. Luck.

My bias favors mainstream science. I was vaccinated in Albuquerque and wore a mask during most interviews. My advice is the result of mainstream reading and reinforced by all I saw and heard along the ride.

My best guess is that it's smart to follow mask guidelines with N95 and KN95 masks. Quarantine and distance when recommended. Vaccinate and boost. Read traditional media reports on the best science. Look for corrections in both, by both. Eat, exercise, and live as healthily as you can.

People should support moves for an authoritative, non-partisan source of health information. Vote for people who push to prepare the healthcare system for the next pandemic.

In Gallup, New Mexico, firefighter Jeremy Padilla broke off our interview to jump on his firetruck and drive to an emergency.

We'll always have fires and pandemics. Firefighters are ready with plans and equipment. The tamping down of future pandemics should be like putting out fires.

Bill Gates's book *How to Prevent the Next Pandemic* quotes epidemiologist Larry Brilliant.

"Outbreaks are inevitable, pandemics are optional."

I recommend readers dip into *The Story Cycle* videos on YouTube after reading *Beast of Main Street* because the written word changes the message people are trying to convey. The videos make it easier to notice more. Body language. Tone. Laughter at key moments. The videos add to understanding.

The ride changed me in profound ways too. I saw all that divides us – age, race, education, politics, religion, geography, status and physical well-being. I also saw the need to come together for everything that means anything to us.

I was moving through a time of mounting deaths, illness, and despair. Along with Covid deaths, another statistic was rising during the ride.

The combined death rate by drugs, alcohol, and suicide rose 20 percent during the first year of Covid, more than at any time on record. American life expectancy is still falling while deaths by despair are rising.

People were dying isolated and alone. Weddings, funerals, church services, and sports events were postponed and cancelled. We are social animals but airborne pandemics make an enemy of the lover's kiss.

Covid isn't going away. It's mutating, and we're living with it. People are still dying. Millions of people are grieving.

Covid's long wake is leaving people with health aftershocks. Grieving is killing people like a collective secret horror show.

I asked about Covid but most people had more worrisome health care issues staring them down. It felt like everyone is on a health spectrum and at the far end are the people without the resources to save themselves.

So much of our survival depends on what's happening in our heads, I wondered where cold, hard calculation starts and imagination starts. The original road trip writer Geoffrey Chaucer noticed this too in the telling of *The Canterbury Tales*, "people can die of mere imagination."

I went through my own existential battle during the writing of the book. At times, all the input my poor brain was receiving was from people suffering loss and mortal dread.

Yet I was not sick and I'm a positive person by nature. I felt the hopeful vitality of the street and knew it was an honor to be alive.

I rode more than 2,500 miles through snow, ice, wind, and rain across eight states. I survived five bicycle breakdowns with the help of the humane actions by others.

Acts of kindness and generosity dominated the trip and the pandemic.

Bicycling was the best way to get out of my information bubble and revive one's faith in humanity.

The whole human comedy and tragedy are heard in the voices of people. Pulitzer Prize-winning author Studs Terkel called it *vox populi,* Latin for voice of the people. Irish author James Joyce said God is, "A shout in the streets."

The truth is we are all riding in the dark on an ancient cycle and the light up ahead may be a truck or the dawn.

The surprises come while riding at dawn through a white fog in the Ozark Mountains listening to the sounds of forests. They come during sublime and bizarre moments like riding next to a cattle stampede or getting lost in a snowstorm on the Great Divide.

I find wonder in the way people think and feel. A young mother from the Acoma Pueblo worried for everyone else during Covid, downplaying her own courage as a single mom fighting mountain wildfires.

A child on a small town square under a hot dog giant was never afraid of dying but he was afraid of losing his grandparents.

I met people I call artists of the air. A tearful 82nd Airborne veteran painted a picture in words, of a dying man reaching out with his hand toward his fiancé outside the window. A bluesman could only say how he felt in a song.

A retired couple in the desert sang magical songs that raised a Lazarus rider back to life in the *Moby Dick* of American pandemics.

In flashes of pain and wonder these moments made up the road I took. Nobody understands it all but you're a lucky one if you're grateful for the ride.

Throughout the ride, I thought the man vs. nature themes in *Moby*

Dick aligned well with the elusive, deadly pandemic and the sublime nature I witnessed along the Route 66 corridor. So much so, I named my bicycle after a doomed whaler.

The original ending of *Moby Dick* called for the white whale to ram the Pequod and the ship goes down with all onboard. British critics complained that a narrator must live to tell the tale.

Succumbing to critical pressure, Herman Melville rewrote the ending for the American audience and it became perhaps the greatest ending in all of American fiction.

In the final version, the Pequod goes down, and then up out of the tumultuous sea pops a painted coffin. All those on board are lost save one. A single man, you can call him Ishmael, grabs hold of the coffin like a buoy.

The coffin symbolizes rebirth and hope. The meaning of the white whale and the madness of humankind depends on multiple subjective perspectives.

I be the collector of perspectives and the stories of coffins and pandemics. Along a road not a road anymore, witness the ways of pandemics and people.

ACKNOWLEDGMENTS

I thank these people with all my heart.

Digital Humanities Production Coordinator Deborah Hendricks at the University of Florida's Samuel Proctor Oral History Program edited all 100-plus videos and recorded disclaimers. She was a dream come true for *The Story Cycle*.

SPOHP Director Dr. Paul Ortiz gave his final approval to the project. My heartfelt thanks.

I caught publicist Lynda O'Connor's enthusiasm. It was infectious.

Chicago Tribune columnist, WGN-Radio host, and Chicago Literary Hall of Famer Rick Kogan was a well of inspiration and support.

Reader Reviews are vital to the success of *Beast of Main Street*. Please review at Goodreads or your favorite book buying site.

PANDEMIC READING LIST

When the book grew in metaphysical scope, reading and soul searching helped.

Favorites: Kurt Anderson, *Fantasyland, The Great Influenza*; Rutger Bregman, *Humankind;* Ian Brenner, *The Power of Crisis*; Manuel Castells, *The Information Age*; Nicholas Christakis, *Apollo's Arrow*; Angus Deaton and Ann Case, *Deaths of Despair*; Jordan Ellenberg, *Shape*; Bill Gates, *How to Prevent the Next Pandemic*; Sam Harris, *Making Sense*; Jamie Holmes, *Nonsense*; Dr. Sabine Hossenfelder; Daniel Kahneman, *Noise*; David McRaney, *How Minds Change*; Michael T. Osterholm, *Deadliest Enemy*; Sara Manning Peskin, *A Molecule Away from Madness*; Steven Pinker, *Rationality*; Joseph Stiglitz, *The Price of Inequality*; Steven Taylor, *Psychology of Pandemics;* and Studs Terkel's *Working*.

Reader Reviews of *Beast of Main Street* are sincerely requested. Support this original concept and new angle on these times. Please review at Goodreads or your favorite book buying site.

ABOUT THE AUTHOR

Michael Sean Comerford is an award-winning former international journalist and author of the bestselling *American OZ: An Astonishing Year in Traveling Carnivals at State Fairs & Festivals - Hitchhiking from California to New York, Alaska to Mexico.*

He's studied Buddhism in the Himalayas, won a heavyweight boxing championship in Ireland, rode freight trains and herded cattle out West, danced a jig in the Amazon and hitchhiked across America, Europe, the Middle East and North Africa.

He lives in Greater Los Angeles to be near his high school-aged daughter Grace Comerford. She's the author of four books.

Reader Reviews are easy, free and super important to the success of *Beast of Main Street*. Please review at Goodreads or your favorite book buying site.

CPSIA information can be obtained
at www.ICGtesting.com
Printed in the USA
LVHW110718221122
733623LV00005B/820